BRITISH RAILWAY
STATION ARCHITECTURE IN COLOUR

For the Modeller and Historian

Robert Hendry

Ian Allan
PUBLISHING

CONTENTS

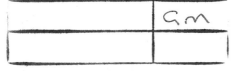
First published 2007

ISBN (10) 0 7110 3282 3
ISBN (13) 0 7110 3282 8

Published by Ian Allan Publishing

an imprint of Ian Allan Publishing Ltd, Hersham, Surrey KT12 4RG.
Printed in England by Ian Allan Printing Ltd, Hersham, Surrey KT12 4RG.

Code: 0712/C

Visit the Ian Allan Publishing website at:
www.ianallanpublishing.com

Title page: Today a rail passenger from Cambridge to Huntingdon must make a detour via March or Hitchin, but this gentle countryside was once served by various cross-country routes built by the Great Eastern Railway and the Great Northern Railway. Sadly they fell victim to rising costs and falling receipts as motor competition increased. St Ives, Huntingdonshire, is a pleasant town with a population of 3,000 people lying 6 miles east of the county town of Huntingdon. For many years, three separate lines approached St Ives. Two came in from the east. Both were owned by the Great Eastern Railway, and diverged from the GER Cambridge – Ely – King's Lynn route, one leaving the main line at Chesterton Junction just north of Cambridge, the other from just south of Ely, forming a triangle with St Ives at the apex. A Great Northern & Great Eastern Joint line approached the town from Huntingdon. Joint Line trains from the west continued on towards Ely as far as Needingworth Junction, a short distance outside St Ives, where the GN & GE joint line turned north towards March. The Ely line lost passenger services as early as 2 February 1931, the Huntingdon line following in 1959. Passenger services through Somersham and Chatteris on the March line ended in 1967, and the Cambridge – St Ives service was the last to go on 5 October 1970. We see St Ives Junction in October 1970, with the GE Type 5 signal box in the foreground, a design that was current from 1884 to 1889. With trains no longer requiring to cross, and confined to DMUs, the far platform was not needed, so the line was used to store freight stock, as there was a vast surplus of 16-ton mineral wagons with the fall in domestic coal consumption, and the growth of Merry-Go-Round services. The slotted concrete signal post on the left is the disused starting signal from the Huntingdon platform, and reminds us that the LNER made considerable use of concrete post signals.

Opposite page: My father was born on Merseyside in 1912. Although his family had close connections with the Isle of Man, and later moved to Rugby, he had a soft spot for Merseyside. When I was a child we sometimes visited Birkenhead, and he pointed out the lettering on the great tower at Hamilton Square station. The white lettering was easy to read, but he told me to look below it, and sure enough, there was more, and I read, 'MERSEY RAILWAY FREQUENT SERVICE OF ELECTRIC TRAINS TO LIVERPOOL &c'. He told me about the Mersey Railway, which burrowed under the river to connect Liverpool and Birkenhead, and had been an independent company until 1948 when it was absorbed into BR. It had been formally opened by HRH The Prince of Wales, later King Edward VII, on 20 January 1886, and was steam worked, but so oppressive did the atmosphere become, that many passengers forsook the trains for the bracing atmosphere of the legendary Mersey ferries. Facing ruin, the only solution was electrification, which was accomplished in 1903 under the supervision of a brilliant young electrical engineer called Joshua Shaw, who later became general manager. In the 1930s, when my father was a student, he called at the Mersey Railway offices to ask if he could look round. He was shown into the office of an elderly gentleman. He seemed unsympathetic, but asked my father where he was from. He replied that he had been born on Merseyside, but had family connections with the Isle of Man, and the elderly gentleman asked him a few questions about the Island and then stood up. My father assumed he was to be shown out of the door; instead he was shown round Birkenhead Central station and the car sheds that adjoined it. His guide was Joshua Shaw, the man who had electrified it thirty years before. It so happened that before Shaw came to the Mersey Railway, he had built another electric railway. It was called the Isle of Man Tramways & Electric Power Co. I decided the frontispiece for this book had to be the 120 foot high hydraulic tower at Hamilton Square station which was built as a triumphal tower to commemorate the creation of rails beneath the Mersey, and to provide a head of water to operate the hydraulic lifts that moved passengers between street level and the trains, some 90 feet below ground level. We see the hydraulic tower, which was built in 1886 to the designs of G E Grayson, in August 1990, the last occasion that my father visited Birkenhead.

Front cover upper: Although the locomotives of the steam age have long gone to the scrap heap or to museums, an array of buildings from the pre-grouping era survived into modern times, offering a welcome link with the legendary names of nineteenth century railways. At Chester Road, in the West Midlands, this modular timber building, that dated from soon after the opening of the line at the start of the 1860s, survived for well over a century. It was built at the start of Sir Richard Moon's long reign as chairman of the London & North Western Railway. Modern writers have castigated Moon as a skinflint, but what he actually did was to give his shareholders a good return whilst providing services that were equal to or superior to his competitors.

Front cover lower: The newest station to be covered in this book is Hastings, where we see the new building in September 2006, a few days prior to its formal opening. One of the fascinating aspects of railways is that a train may depart from a 21st century station and in minutes be running into a station that was built before Queen Victoria came to the throne.

Rear cover: The front cover illustrations portrayed an 1860s LNWR modular timber building and the new station at Hastings that was formally opened in 2006. For our final scene, I have selected the Metropolitan Railway terminus at Croxley, which was opened in 1925. It was built to the Domestic Revival style which was popular in the early years of the twentieth century, and was designed by Charles W Clark, the Metropolitan Railway architect.

Opposite page top: Recently, a bus enthusiast remarked that even with Black and White TV in the 1960s, if a news item showed a street scene and buses, he could identify most large towns or cities by the buses, without having the sound on, but this would no longer be the case. The same was true of railways. A glance at a photograph of a station was often sufficient to identify the company. This view of Droitwich, taken on 2 July 1976, demonstrates the point. The GWR balanced arm signals, which were used where signal siting was awkward, are an immediate answer, but so is the GWR signal box in the distance. The station building shouts Great Western, and is to a pattern that spread after the Badminton and South Wales cut-off opened in 1902. The Gents toilet with the louvered roof and three end windows, the centre window being wider than the other two, was also found at Calne, and Badminton itself, to give but two examples. A view of the end wall would identify the hand of the Great Western. The canopy is equally revealing. Apart from such give-aways, there were lesser clues, and with the wholesale destruction of mechanical signalling and the demolition of many buildings, it can be the smaller items that provide an answer today. They include footbridges, railings, fences and lineside huts. The view on the title page shows a signal box at St Ives. The GWR also served St Ives, but that was St Ives in Cornwall, not in Huntingdonshire, but no well-informed observer could mistake one station for the other, even if he had never visited either town.

Opposite page bottom: A photograph can be seen through many eyes, as this view demonstrates. The mellow light and autumn tints in this 1980 portrait of Sutton Coldfield station are undeniably attractive. The sharply curved platforms would appeal to the artist as they break up the tyranny of the conventional vanishing point that dominates most pictures. The row of supports for the canopy on the right is pleasing, whilst the trees and buildings on the skyline set off the rising ground in the background. The only gap is the lack of a matching building on the other platform. Had a spectator stood here on the early afternoon of Sunday 23 January 1955, the scene would have been little changed, save for a building on the down platform. Had our spectator lingered, he might have heard the beat of an express train approaching fast from the north. Sutton was not an express route, but was used for diversions when engineering works blocked other routes. Such was the case on that Sunday afternoon. Because of the sharp curve, there was a 30 mph speed restriction, but for some reason, the conductor-driver, who had been selected for his route knowledge for the 12.15 York – Bristol express, entered the station at 55-60 mph. The train derailed, sweeping away the station buildings on the down platform, and claiming 17 lives. The driver died, so no explanation for this tragedy has ever been forthcoming. The curve that makes the location so pleasing to the photographer, was an inconvenience to the operating department, and when the driver of a fast train miscalculated, led to tragedy.

INTRODUCTION

A few days before I started work on this book, my wife and I visited a small country station in Kent. So often one finds a couple of 'bus shelters', but this time one of the original buildings survived. As I photographed it, a couple from the antipodes, who were waiting for a train, asked if I knew how old it was. I said it dated from the 1850s. Few buildings in New Zealand date back that far, and we chatted briefly. That conversation sparked a train of thought that has influenced this book. Some of the men who built it would have been born before Napoleon Bonaparte or Horatio Nelson rose to fame. Whilst the train we were about to photograph was a product of the twenty-first century, it was passing a structure that men from the eighteenth century would have known. It was a fascinating reflection that I was seeing this juxtaposition of continuity and change and a link with generations who were born when the fastest mode of transport was the galloping horse.

Looking at another station, I could see how it had been enlarged and altered in pre-grouping days, with extensions that were a good but not a perfect match, and how the Southern Railway had made improvements, so that the railings protecting the subway differed on both platforms. British Railways had made further alterations, and Railtrack and Network Rail had continued the process. This offered another theme. Victorian locomotive engineers carried out some amazing transformations with locomotives, for did not the GWR convert some broad gauge 0-4-2T locomotives into standard gauge 4-4-0 tender engines, yet no locomotive engineer had accomplished such dramatic adaptations as generations of railway civil engineers regarded as routine. When a line opened, a station might serve a small village, which, under the stimulus of the railway age, grew into a large town. Unless he could start afresh on a green field site, which was rare, the Civil Engineer had to adapt an existing site to cater for several times the traffic, and to meet rising expectations as well, as low platforms gave way to full height platforms, and footbridges and canopies became routine. Goods facilities that were acceptable in 1840 might be overtaxed within years. The Civil Engineer met these calls, and unlike the railway of today, where weekend engineering disruption and closures are routine, as is occasional total closure for days or weeks, traffic had to keep moving. To put it into a motive power context, it is as if a locomotive engineer was told to convert Stephenson's *Rocket* into a 25kV electric capable of hauling a 1000-ton train, and to keep it in service whilst doing so.

Continuity and Change were obvious themes, and having referred to locomotive engineers, this brings in another feature. If you were to place photographs of Stroudley, Churchward and Bulleid engines before an enthusiast, most could identify the products of each of these talented men, and many enthusiasts would be able to reel off a list of locomotive engineers. Although their engines have long since gone for scrap or for preservation, we know of the great steam engi-

neers, but who were the contemporary civil engineers and architects, whose heritage still survives? Over the years, I have discovered a little about them. They include John Foster, Frederick Barnes, Francis Thompson, Sir William Tite, or Donald Matheson, and one name that will be familiar to every reader, Isambard Kingdom Brunel. Although some stations can be attributed to a specific designer, often this is not possible, and they slip into the anonymity of the Chief Civil Engineer's office where a nameless draftsman shaped a building that was to outlast him by generations. Even with this sad qualification, the cast list is remarkable, and adds to the story. As a youngster, I read about Stanier or Stroudley, but books were silent on Livock or Miller. Finding out about them was a voyage of discovery, and I hope you will enjoy reading of them, as much as I enjoyed the search.

The question, 'What is a Railway Station?' may seem superfluous, as most people would say they can recognise a station, but this is due to our familiarity with the railway station of today. When the railway age dawned, this was possible, as the station had to evolve along with everything else. A railway exists to move goods or people from place to place, and a station is the place where they are loaded or unloaded. In modern parlance, it is the interface between the customer and the train. The earliest practical railways were in the coalfields in the North East, and connected the collieries with the ports to facilitate the movement of coal to the coastal ships that moved it over long distances. The first 'stations' were collieries and coal staithes. This may seem confusing, as we now class such installations as private sidings, rather than as stations, as they cater for the traffic of one particular user, and are not open to the public, but if we ignore this, we fail to understand how stations evolved. The Stockton & Darlington Railway of 1825, which was the first practical railway, was a coal mover, and passenger traffic was an afterthought. It was not until the Liverpool & Manchester Railway in 1830 that the modern intercity railway appeared, with recognised passenger stations. Except at major termini, the passenger station had a small building that served the same purpose as the coaching inns in the days of the stagecoach, and early stations and passenger carriages drew on the expertise of the coaching trade. Passengers boarded the stagecoach from ground level, and the same facilities were provided now that it ran on flanged wheels. Within a few years, raised platforms had evolved, and the ground level platform was replaced by a low platform that increased in height until the high platform of today with level access to the carriage.

Armed with that thought, we realise that station design has evolved to meet traffic and legal requirements, as railways have responded to their customers' demands, and have been subject to a tight legislative framework. There have been positive and negative factors. In the nineteenth century, most were positive. In the twentieth century, the growth of motor vehicles took traffic away from the railways and led to massive closures from 1950 onwards, and the need to cut costs prompted the removal of many facilities that were once taken for granted. Vandalism is a curse of modern life and many facilities that could otherwise have survived have been lost because of a minority of social misfits. Until our politicians punish such behaviour forcefully, rather than talk mindlessly, this can only get worse, and politicians will only do so when voter reaction makes them fear for their seats. In recent times, public demand for better facilities for the disabled and the growth of a compensation culture, where lawyers can tout for compensation business on TV, has impacted on stations.

In this book, we will explore some stations from the dawn of the railway age, and see how the modern station evolved between 1830 and 1850. It was an era of boundless self-confidence, indicated by some of the magnificent Classical, Tudor or Jacobean stations that sprang up. England had emerged triumphant from the Napoleonic wars, and was set on the road to imperial grandeur. Classical architecture that recalled the glories of Imperial Rome and ancient Greece, seemed fitting. In this, the railways reflected the taste of their day. Tudor and Jacobean themes reflected a growing admiration for the stirring days of Queen Elizabeth 1st, or the romance of the Stuart era. Railways were subject to these national trends, and station design reflected the growing self-confidence of Britain, and the feeling that the railway was a great new force. At first, stations were compact, and even major termini, such as Euston, were small, a problem that later became acute, as stations had to grow piecemeal. Points were hand worked, and fixed signals were non-existent. By the 1840s, the first concentration of point levers had taken place, and fixed semaphore signals made their appearance. The Board of Trade demanded concentration of point levers and interlocking on new lines, or when existing stations were remodelled, and imposed limits on the distance at which points could be worked from a box on passenger lines. As an alternative to points, small turntables were used to marshal the short four-wheel carriages, with wagon turntables in goods yards. In a small goods yard, a single siding was reached via a trailing point off the main line and wagon turntables would permit sidings to radiate out from this. The increasing size of coaching stock soon eliminated the coach turntable, but the wagon turntable survived into BR days.

These trends continued into our next period, from 1850 to 1875. By now, most main lines were well established, along with the large companies that were to dominate the railway scene until 1923. New main lines appeared, but the main emphasis was on infilling and secondary routes, and the need to cope with rapid expansion on the main lines. Classical themes were waning by the 1860s, but station design remained magnificent. When the Midland Railway entered London, it selected the most prestigious of all British architects, Sir George Gilbert Scott, to design the fantastic Gothic frontage for St Pancras station, the ultimate manifestation of high Victorian confidence. Even so, St Pancras was an anachronism, as high Victorian Gothic was facing challenges as a building style. Although lavish stations might have prestige value, or be necessary to conciliate a powerful and intransigent nobleman, rising costs were forcing a more realistic approach by the 1870s. Railway managers increasingly sought a more economical policy. Sir Richard Moon, the powerful chairman of the London & North Western Railway has been characterised by generations of writers as an austere unfeeling skinflint. In fact, Moon wanted value for money and set his face against unnecessary ornamentation, as a study of pre-Moon and Moon era structures reveals. Under Moon and the superb team of officers he built up, the LNWR provided cheap but durable solutions to its operating problems, one of which was the development of a range of pre-fabricated wooden buildings that could be erected cheaply yet do the job admirably. Although using brick, the GWR adopted a similar policy of standardised buildings and components under Lancaster Owen, a capable and talented engineer, so Moon was not alone in following this course.

After 1890, the trend towards economy intensified, and the LNWR was to the forefront with basic buildings for minor stations where magnificent stone or brick structures would once have been provided. On the bigger companies, the 1870s and 1880s saw a rapid extension of absolute block working and interlocking of signals and points, and this, coupled with the distance rules on working points produced a clear pattern in station design. At small country stations, the yard was beyond the platforms at one end of the station, reached via trailing connections off the running lines. The signal box was at the end of the platform, or if the yard was long, part way along, to keep within the distance rules. If there was a level crossing, the box would be at the crossing, or a separate small box or ground frame would be provided. At larger stations, the rules on the distance at which points might be worked made it impossible to use one box, so there would be a signal box at each end of the station. Large stations, such as Leicester (London Road), Rugby or Crewe, might have intermediate platform boxes as well, and boxes further out, so that trains were signalled by a succession of boxes. The Armagh accident in June 1889, when a train stalled on a bank, and was divided, the rear portion running away and colliding with a second train worked on the time interval system, shocked the country, and led to the Regulation of Railways Act 1889, which made interlocking, block signalling, and continuous brakes on passenger trains compulsory. This compelled the laggard companies to catch up, but only speeded up a process that was well advanced.

Traffic continued to increase in the 1880s and 1890s, with quadrupling completed on most of the main routes out of London. At the close of the Nineteenth century, the most prestigious railway project was the Great Central Railway 'London Extension', though the West Highland and West Highland Extension railways in Scotland had an even greater romantic appeal. The Light Railways Act of 1896 prompted a flurry of cheaply built rural lines at the close of the nineteenth century, and in the early years of the twentieth century. In 1900, the railways of Britain seemed to have reached the zenith of their power and prestige. Although economy was to the fore where traffic prospects were poor, in locations where heavy or prestige traffic was expected, stations reached a new pinnacle of excellence, as at Wemyss Bay in Scotland, which was the work of one of the most outstanding railway engineers of the age, Donald A Matheson, engineer-in-chief of the Caledonian Railway. Port St Mary station, in the Isle of Man was another example of turn of the century magnificence. Dating from 1898, it was a far cry from the wood and corrugated iron huts provided when the Isle of Man Railway opened in the 1870s, and was an indication of how wealthy and confident the successful companies had become. This was not surprising as their only rivals were coastal shipping for slow moving mineral traffic, the canals which were a dying force, and the horse drawn carriers' cart, which was used to connect with the local station, but was not suitable for long distance movement. The first motor vehicles were spluttering about the roads, and in the early 1900s, the railway companies were amongst the earliest providers of bus services as feeders to existing railway lines, but few people saw the motor vehicle as a serious threat.

If there was a problem in 1900, it was not the motor vehicle, but the electric tramcar that was abstracting short haul inner city passenger traffic. This led to a brief boom in steam railcar construction, most of which were useless, save for examples produced by the GWR, LNWR and Lancashire & Yorkshire Railway. The GWR, with 99 cars, extended them to country areas, opening many wayside halts, as did the LNWR. Railway officers were also concerned at the growing strength of the union movement, and by 1907, labour unrest had become a major factor. Several disputes, and the threats of rail strikes, placed pressure on operating costs, whilst the new electric tramways continued to erode short distance traffic in the big cities. The years from 1900, although a Golden Age, offered a warning of what might happen in time. The 'Domestic Revival' school of architects enjoyed success at the close of the Nineteenth Century, and in the Edwardian era. Art Nouveau made its appearance, as did other styles, which made the remaining years up to 1914 interesting. The Great War, from 1914 to 1918, disrupted every aspect of life, and apart from costing millions of casualties, impoverished Europe for a generation, and transformed social, economic and political life beyond recognition. War deflected attention from domestic issues, and the impact of a brief postwar boom, recession, inflation and labour unrest created havoc with railway finances. Parliament had resolutely opposed railway amalgamation up to 1914, but after 1918, did an about-face, forcing the grouping on to the railway industry, with the 120 or so major companies forcibly merged into the Big Four in 1923. It was a shotgun marriage, and like many such unions was not happy. It also presaged an era of catastrophic political meddling with railways that has continued unabated into modern times.

Our next period opens in 1923, although much of the development over the few years was the residue of pre-grouping schemes. By 1925, the Big Four were developing policies of their own and this included new architectural trends, most notably the Southern adoption of the New Classical style, and subsequently Art Deco. In the 1920s, Victorian design was reviled as fussy and over complicated; in the 1950s, New Classical and Art Deco styles were similarly reviled, but today we can look back at many fine structures from both periods. The LMS and LNER also embraced modernism, but with less panache than the Southern to begin with. The Great Western, which had retained its identity in 1923, merely absorbed its smaller neighbours, and was the most conservative of the Big Four. Even so, it produced one of the most memorable buildings of the new era during the rebuilding of the decaying Brunellian station at Leamington Spa in 1938. In this introduction, we see how railway architecture adopted contemporary styles, and this characterised the 1920s and 1930s. Indeed, some of the finest Interwar buildings were railway structures. The war placed the railways under new strains, and generated much additional traffic. Mostly this was handled at existing stations, but in a few places new stations were provided. Wartime urgency and austerity meant they were basic, as at Canley Gates. The period from 1939 to 1945 saw massive destruction of the network through the German bomber offensive, and overuse, and because of government policy, railways came low in the queue for materials after 1945. Understandably the period from 1939 to 1947 contributed little of merit to station design through no fault of the railway companies.

The advent of a Labour government that was committed to Nationalisation in 1945 spelled the end for the Big Four, and in 1948, British Railways came into being, and this heralds the start of our next section. BR inherited all the problems of the old companies. Far from being a golden age, as the politicians trumpeted, closer political interference with a nationalised industry meant that electoral advantage became a potent factor in railway planning, and BR found itself unpopular with politicians of all political complexions. A lunatic financial structure, which I have covered in depth in *The Changing Face of Britain's Railways 1938–1953*, created an apparent deficit that soon turned into a real deficit, and politicians, though profligate wasters of money, are sensitive to accusations of being wasteful, so demanded that railwaymen do something. The order, 'Do something' usually means that the speaker has no idea of what to do, and this was the case with the politicians after 1948. This led to the first closures, to the Modernisation Plan of 1955, which was then speeded up with catastrophic results, and finally to the Beeching Plan of 1963, with the closure of thousands of miles of line, and of thousands of stations. The railway network was too extensive for the motor age, and however sad it was, many lines were rightly closed, but once rationalisation became accepted, the process went too far, and if necessary, figures were massaged to give the right answer. New or rebuilt stations appeared, as at West Ruislip or Coventry, but except for selected main lines where modernisation was the word, the main theme was retrenchment. Under the direction of the Chief Architect of British Railways, Dr F F C Curtis, the predominant architectural style was Modernism. The Beeching process continued for some time after Dr Beeching's retirement. The pace of closures eventually slowed down, whilst some important new stations appeared, such as Birmingham International. Stations re-opened on existing lines where hasty Beeching era closures were seen as a mistake, and a few lines that had closed to passengers were re-opened. Although the creation of British Railways in 1948 created

one gigantic monolith from Cornwall to Caithness, the railways of Ireland, which had been subject to similar influences from the 1830s onwards, were outside BR, and as in previous volumes, I have looked at the British Isles as a whole rather than just BR, as there is much to be discovered from such comparisons. Belfast Central, a completely new station that resurrected a mid-Victorian idea is an example. Privatisation in the 1990s led to a chaotic railway industry, with the infrastructure owned by Railtrack, which was replaced by Network Rail, but with train services and many stations being the responsibility of Train Operating Companies, or TOCs.

Each age tends to look on the period immediately preceding it with disdain, as is apparent with architecture, but as an era moves further into the past, the virtues of its architecture become more apparent. Edwardians reviled mid Victorian architecture, whilst Edwardian style was abhorred by the modernists in the 1930s. They in turn were derided in the fifties. Today we see merit in all these periods, whilst 1960s modernist architecture is generally held in contempt. If historic precedent holds good, that period will come into its own in another twenty to thirty years, but the low quality of construction of many postwar buildings, and the obsessive pursuit of modernity to the point at which aesthetics, durability or convenience to the user become meaningless, has left a legacy of buildings that have aged prematurely. Many 1850s houses or stations are still sound. Many 1960s blocks of flats have been demolished. Paradoxically this pursuit of newness and difference resulted in an internationalisation of design to the point at which a building could just as well be a tax office in California, a school in Wales, or a railway station in Germany. The quality of each of the periods I have covered up to 1939 is now appreciated. It is too early to say whether this will apply to the Modernist architecture, or whether this period will prove to be the exception to the rule, save for an occasional outstanding structure.

The start and end point of each period is, of necessity, arbitrary, and different trends became apparent at different times on different companies. I could find exceptions that prove the start point for each period should be later, but other exceptions suggest the opposite. In general, this analysis offers a convenient framework. If we see a station that is out of period, it helps us to realise this, and encourages us to ask why. Fifty years ago, when I was a child, thousands of stations existed that have been lost forever. This is sad, but even today, there is a rich tapestry to explore. I can look at the incredible splendour of St Pancras, one of the most extravagant fairy palaces of all time, or I can revel in the 1926 Southern New Classicism at Ramsgate. Both are superb. I can recall tiny country stations on main lines, where a procession of express trains roared through, but a stopping train was an event. It was a fascinating world, and I am glad I knew it first hand. In describing stations and the communities they served, I have made occasional reference to population, to give some idea of the traffic the station handled. A uniform date seemed better than random dates, to permit comparisons on a level playing field, and I selected 1951. The stations in this volume mostly opened between 1830 and

1935, so any date before the 1941 census could not be universal, and 1941 was distorted by war. Most of the railway system still survived in 1951, but much has gone since then, so 1951 seemed to be optimum. When describing Flint station in North Wales, I have compared it to Llandudno, to make the point that seaside resorts might have a small resident population, but a large visiting population, so population is not an infallible guide to how a station develops.

The loss of many historic stations is sad, and few today would condone the official vandalism that led to the destruction of the Doric Arch or the Great Hall at Euston, both of which were architectural gems. We hear comments that these were in the bad old days, and that in this more enlightened age, it could not happen again, but in 1976, my father and I visited Derby, where the frontage of the 1839–1841 'Tri-Junct' station still stood. Although substantially altered over the years, it was an historic structure, and with its Wyverns, an imposing presence in the town. It was later swept away in a repeat of the vandalism that had seen the demise of the Doric arch. Again, we hear voices that it could not happen nowadays. In 1931, J R Scott designed a remarkable octagonal booking office that included a contemporary art deco frieze at Hastings. Sadly the frieze was removed in the 1960s, but worse was to follow in 2004. An officially backed redevelopment project for the station and its approaches took place, and to prevent any last minute listing of this important 1930s building, Railtrack obtained an immunity from listing, so that conservationists would be unable to protect our heritage. The moral of this story seems clear, that the official vandalism that destroyed the Great Hall or Derby station is alive and flourishing. Despite its important contribution to 1930s architecture, Hastings did not have adequate listed protection, and by the time anyone realised that, it was too late. We ignore those lessons at our peril and to the detriment of future generations, and if this book alerts readers to that threat to our heritage, I shall be well content.

One other point is worth mentioning. In 1976, Sir Peter Parker, who was one of the most articulate of BR chairmen, commented, 'The drive to modernise existing stations to improve passenger environment is hampered by the number of 'listed' stations which the Board owns'. At that time, the number of listed structures on BR stood at 486, and has risen massively since then. A station's purpose is to provide an interface between the passenger and the train, and BR and its successors have at times pointed out that restoration can be more costly than starting from scratch. Unless the state or local authorities contribute to such costs, the only way they can be met is by passing them on to the consumer. As listing is intended to conserve the heritage that we all benefit from, it is questionable if such costs should be levied on the passenger. We share the costs of education across the whole of society, rather than say that it must be borne by parents alone, and this principle applies in many other fields. The railway industry has an exceptional number of outstanding buildings, so it is right that it has a high number of listed structures, but it may be that the present listing process, which benefits the community in protecting our heritage, but is a financial millstone to the owner of any listed property, requires overhaul. Some years ago, when one structure was listed, BR responded by demolishing several comparable buildings almost overnight. One albatross was a nuisance; several would have been intolerable. As a conservationist, I deplore this, but it made good economic sense, and I find it hard to condemn them for doing what any sane person would do in that situation. Is a system that punishes a property owner who has conserved his property for decades fair or sensible? That is what our present system does. Vigilance is important, but so is an effective and fair conservation policy. We have neither.

This series commenced with a book on wagons in 1999, and everyone thought we were crazy to cover such a specialised subject in colour, but it required a reprint within twelve months. The series now covers wagons, coaches, signalling, infrastructure and stations. The first volume in the Stations range was written by the late Nick Jardine. Sadly Nick passed away recently, so I have been invited to write this volume, building on the excellent start made by Nick. I would like to pay tribute to Nick for his pioneering work in the Stations series. As stations form part of the overall railway infrastructure, they also received attention in 'British Railway Infrastructure in Colour', and the views in this volume have been selected to complement rather than duplicate material in that book. In this volume, I have concentrated on Station Architecture, although many views showing trackwork, signalling and other features appear, and at Leicester London Road, I have shown how the physical constraints of the site affected the shape of the station, and the way it was worked.

Most railway enthusiasts are interested in motive power, but an interest in stations is less common, and I owe my initial interest in railway stations to my father, Dr Robert Preston Hendry (1912–1991). He was a 'railway enthusiast' in the sense of being interested in the overall railway scene. He was interested in how each component interacted to create a harmonious whole. Without motive power, the trains could not run; without tracks there would be no smooth way for them; without stations and goods depots, there would be no place to receive and discharge their load of passengers and freight; without signalling, safety would be lacking. To my father, the station was as much a part of the railway scene as the locomotive. He wished to film the railway infrastructure that he had grown up with. Material has come from the colour archive he started in the 1950s when colour photography of steam locomotives was a minority interest, and colour photography of stations was a minority within a minority. I wish I could say how many stations I have visited since then, but it must run into four figures. One year, my father and I kept a running count of the stations we visited, and I photographed him standing on the platform at our 150th station of that year, but I lost count before the year was over. Even with that rate of progress, our visits have barely scratched the surface of what is a vast subject, as the BR Annual Report and Accounts for 1948 reveals only too clearly. On 1 January 1948, BR inherited 1,886 passenger only stations, 4,815 passenger and freight sta-

tions, and 1,593 freight only stations, a grand total of 8,294. If it were possible to cover every station with one view, the resultant book would require a crane to lift it.

Within 96 pages, selection is inevitable, and if space is allowed for a reasonable size for each illustration, about 160 views are feasible. The statistician may work out that with one photo per station, we would require 51.83 volumes to cover the railways of the UK mainland. Would one photo per station be wise? I think not, for whilst this would cover the maximum number of sites, many stations deserve more than one view, and much of the depth of the subject would be lost. In selecting material, I have covered stations from the dawn of railways to modern times, and from the South of England to the North of Scotland, and from East Anglia to the Emerald Isle. I have examined the work of some of the great designers, and covered stations varying from small halts to important city stations. One such example is Leicester (London Road) with seven views. Even then, I have had to cull some views, but to have included them would have meant omissions elsewhere. Why do we need so many views? It is a complex station with an outstanding frontage on London Road, and the signalling and working practices of a large station were little understood by most enthusiasts even in steam days, and with the mechanical signalling era receding into the past, it is helpful to examine how such stations were signalled. Even with omissions, we have used seven views to cover a distance of 600 yards, or 20 views per mile, and on that level of cover, we would require over ½m illustrations, which would fill over 3,000 volumes. To chart the right course is difficult, for there is no ideal answer, and every author, if asked how many pages he wanted, would reply 'more'. A reader modelling a specific station would also want more of 'his' station. If the reader feels that a specific station, company or engineer merited inclusion, I would probably agree. My problem has been that the only way it could have been included would have been to omit something else. If this volume receives the same response from readers that others in this series have been given, maybe there will be a sequel though I doubt that we will get to 51.83 volumes, let alone 3,000!

Without the assistance of many people, this book would not have been possible. First and foremost, I would like to acknowledge my debt to my father, Dr Robert Preston Hendry, who passed his interest in railways on to me. As a general practitioner, he had to observe humanity to diagnose the illnesses in his patients, and those powers were applied in other fields such as railways, where he often asked the question, 'why is it like this, and what does it tell us'. Another maxim he applied was, 'Don't guess, find out', and that was as valuable in understanding railway stations as with patients. My mother felt this interest in railways was good for a youngster, as it embraced geography, history, economics, and many other subjects. She accepted that family outings would often include a visit to a railway station, sometimes by train, but often by car to the less frequently served locations. This prompted a family joke that with her unrivalled experience of station car parks, she would write the definitive his-

tory of the railway station car park. Sadly this was not to be, but station car parks do appear in this volume, so perhaps a true word was spoken in jest. In recent years, my wife, Elena, who was born in the Soviet Union, where the railway enthusiast was a rarity, has accompanied me on trips. Elena overcame her astonishment that anyone would wish to film a train or a trolleybus, and has developed a keen eye for what is unusual, and has taken some of the views in this book. One school friend who operated my father's model railway, is Clive Partridge, who was to join British Railways, and rise to managerial rank. He has provided a professional railwayman's viewpoint. Finally, I should extend a special thank you to the many station masters, supervisors, area managers, and other officers on British Railways, Railtrack, Network Rail, the Ulster Transport Authority and Northern Ireland Railways, CIE and Irish Rail, who have approved countless visits to stations over a period stretching back more than half a century. Without their co-operation, this book could never have been written.

Opposite page bottom: Apart from the experimental rebuilding of the former MR electrified lines between Lancaster and Morecambe, the electrification of the London Midland main line between Liverpool, Manchester and Euston was the first 25 kV main line electrification in the British Isles, and many technical problems had to be resolved. The section between Manchester and Crewe, much of which came within the Stoke division of the LM Region, was selected as the pilot scheme. As well as electrification itself, with the concomitant provision of motive power and rolling stock, the opportunity was taken to provide a 'modern' railway, upgrading stations and signalling. Years of deferred maintenance during the war, and in the austerity period thereafter, had resulted in many passenger stations being badly rundown, and with electrification and new signalling, there came a desire for a better passenger environment. This could have been accomplished by refurbishing the many fine buildings provided in Victorian days, but the sixties were the era of the 'New Town' dream, in which bright modern architecture would replace outmoded Victorian cities, and BR was susceptible to the vision that gripped architects, town planners and politicians alike. Conservation or 'Heritage' were not 'in' words, and spending money on revamping an old building was seen as negative. If major work was needed, as at Congleton, where a level crossing was to be replaced by a bridge, a new building was seen as the way to project the bright new image that BR wanted. The BR Annual Report records that work at Congleton began in 1963, and was still progressing the following year. The Stoke division of BR was one of the first sections of BR to replace traditional Station masters with Station Managers, a process that began late in 1964, and spread throughout the Division early in 1965, Congleton being one of seven such areas. We see Congleton station in September 1989.

Above: This portrait of the Down buildings at Newport (Mon) in June 1994 symbolises the steady evolution of the railway system. The original South Wales Railway station at Newport dated from 1848/50. In 1878, the GWR massively rebuilt it. Lancaster Owen (1843-1911), who had trained under, and later succeeded his father as Chief Engineer for Construction to the GWR, and J E Danks, who were together responsible for developing a GWR house style for stations in the 1870s, were impressed with the quality of the 1848 station, so incorporated part of the down side buildings in their 1878 rebuild, and constructed the new buildings to match. In 1928, the GWR drastically modified the station at Newport to accommodate the enlarged Newport Divisional offices following the take over of the South Wales valleys lines in 1923. The upper floors are from the later rebuilding, but the ground floor retains the rock faced stone of the 1848 and 1878 stations. However the rectangular windows and concrete lintels are not original, the earlier design comprising tall round headed windows grouped in pairs.

THE FORMATIVE YEARS
1830–1850

Although the Liverpool & Manchester Railway was not the first railway to carry passengers, having been preceded by the Stockton & Darlington by five years, and by the precursor to the Swansea & Mumbles Railway, which had been conveying passengers as early as 1807, the L&M was the first intercity main line where long distance passenger traffic was seen as important, and its opening in 1830 marked the birth of the railway station as we know it. The next twenty years up to 1850 were to see the feeble infant of those days grow into a resourceful and powerful figure. They must have been exciting times.

Below: This pioneering role gives the Liverpool & Manchester Railway a unique niche in railway history, and makes its termini significant. The geography of Liverpool was not conducive to railway building, and the L&M approached the city through a deep rock cutting. At Edge Hill, the line split in two, both lines plunging into tunnels, one climbing to a passenger terminal at Crown Street, the other dropping to a freight terminal at Wapping. Because early locomotives were incapable of hauling trains on a steep gradient, both inclines were cable worked. Engines were detached at Edge Hill, and trains hauled up grade to Crown Street, where the tracks terminated almost at right angles to the street. At the terminus, the single line through the tunnel divided into three, the northern-most track serving a platform, the other two lines being for carriage storage. As locomotive working was not envisaged, there was no need

for run round facilities, so the tracks were connected at the other end of the station by carriage turntables, which were decked with wood. A narrow two story Georgian building of dressed stone was erected, the main entrance being in the end facing Crown Street. A low platform was provided, but this stopped short of the track, and acted as a paved walkway, rather than a platform, access to the trains being from ground level. A canopy supported by twelve columns offered protection from the elements. When the line opened on Wednesday 15 September 1830, this was the sum total of facilities, but a wooden trainshed was added, resting on the canopy supports on one side, and on the perimeter wall on the other side. This view is from an aquatint plate by Thomas Bury and first appeared in 1831, but which exists in several versions. In some prints, the end of the trainshed is open, revealing the roof structure, but others show it with horizontal boarding. Some views show a lean-to to the right of the station; others do not. It is known that the Bury prints were updated in 1831–1833 to reflect progress on the L&M, and to correct errors. Unless the trainshed roof was glazed, and there is no evidence of this, the end cladding would make it very dark. The engine house for the Wapping and Crown Street inclines was located at Edge Hill, so was at the top of the Wapping incline, but at the foot of Crown Street bank, which complicated workings, the cable running from Edge Hill to the far end of Crown Street and then back down to Edge Hill where it was connected to an in-bound train. Only the centre track at Crown Street was provided with guides, but there must have been pulleys at the far end of the station. As the platform line diverged sharply at the tunnel mouth, the cable rubbed against the tunnel portal, and over a century later, this still showed rope burns on the stonework. The

cable was returned down grade on a separate wagon, as trains were not lowered down hill by cable, but gravity worked. *Thomas Bury*

Opposite page top: The station was remote from the city centre on a cramped site bounded by Crown Street on the west, and by the tunnel mouth at the east. The L&M provided a free horse omnibus to and from the city centre, and the cost of this, and the rapid growth of traffic, which the station was ill equipped to cope with, prompted the L&M to consider replacing it within a few months, and the necessary Act of Parliament was secured in 1832. Although not finished, the replacement terminus at Liverpool Lime Street was opened on 15 August 1836, giving Crown Street less than six years as a passenger station. As the Wapping freight facilities were already overtaxed, Crown Street became a goods depot, and with extensions, survived until the 1970s. Alas, the chance of conserving this astonishing relic from the birth of railways was lost when the area was landscaped, and the original tunnel mouth at Crown Street buried, although the remains of a second later tunnel still survive. This track plan, from December 1916, is from the Lancashire Division 'Diagram of Private Sidings' records of the London & North Western Railway, into which the L&M had been absorbed in 1846. This shows that the depot was extended in both directions along Crown Street, although the main extension is to the left of the original track, which runs almost at right angles to Crown Street. On the left, the new property was bounded by Smithdown Lane, and included an agricultural depot and private sidings serving several colliery 'landsale' sidings, whilst Fletcher Burrows yard was to the right. The profusion of wagon turntables is noteworthy, and was a feature of early goods depots, but the layout is extremely awkward to shunt, and with

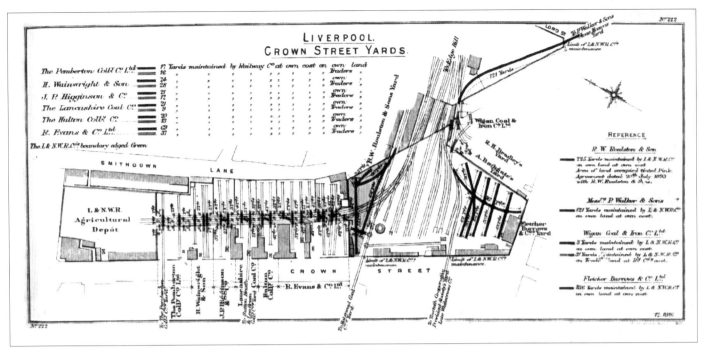

LIVERPOOL.
CROWN STREET YARDS.

Roulston's yard lying across the access to the agricultural depot and other users, this must have been a recipe for trouble. The purpose of these diagrams was to define the track the company maintained, and the track the trader maintained, and who paid for it. At Crown Street, the LNWR maintained track on its own land and on trader's land, due to the compact site and risk of inadequate maintenance by traders interrupting other movements.

Right: The opening of the Liverpool & Manchester Railway in 1830 had been a great event, attended by the Duke of Wellington, but in 1832, powers were obtained for a new tunnel to descend from Edge Hill to Lime Street, where a new terminal that would also accommodate the Grand Junction Railway from Birmingham, was planned. The L&M transferred services to the incomplete Lime Street station on 15 August 1836, but such was Liverpool Council's desire for a magnificent terminal, that the Council agreed to contribute up to £2000. At this date, a grand terminal was seen as an asset to a city, but such generosity was remarkable, and an amazing contrast to later years, when councils saw railways and tramways as a golden goose to be plucked. At times, such avarice backfired, and led to railways building out-of-town stations, and to tramway projects being dropped. Rugby was one such example, where ruthless demands by the council led to a tramway scheme (that had legislative approval) being dropped. With the lack of new railways today, councils sate themselves by a relentless onslaught on the hapless council taxpayer, causing distress to many elderly residents. How little do attitudes change in city hall! Liverpool's positive attitude in the 1830s resulted in a superb frontage that was designed by the Liverpool city surveyor and architect, John Foster, who had succeeded his father to the post in 1824. Foster was responsible for the lavish St George's Hall which faced the station. Instead of the modest road elevation of Crown

Street, Foster created a magnificent façade on Lime Street. With 28 Corinthian columns and a frontage pierced by four equally spaced Roman Triumphal arches, the station was 'the great public entrance into Liverpool' that the L&M wanted. It was faced in Millstone Grit and Devonshire Granite, and captured the mood that the buildings of Ancient Greece and Rome most closely reflected noble and worthy ideals. In five years, the L&M had come a long way from its little station at Crown Street to a classical temple to railways. The new station was to house not just the L&M, but the Grand Junction Railway as well, and a medallion similar to the one issued at the opening of the L&MR marked the event. In 1830, Thomas

Woolfield had offered a medallion in silver, bronze or pewter. His successor, W B Promoli, of Church St, Liverpool, issued a medallion to mark the opening of the GJR on 4 July 1837. The face depicted the Grand Façade of the New Railway Station, Liverpool, whilst the reverse celebrated the Weaver viaduct. The L&B medallion of 1830 had measured 48mm, but the new medallion at 55mm, was bigger. Promoli presented two silver medals to the L&B board. Sadly, this magnificent frontage was swept away in 1865-67 to make way for the North Western Hotel, which although a magnificent building, does not extend the full length of the trainshed that was erected between 1867 and 1874. See page 40.

Above: The Newcastle & Carlisle Railway was authorised on 22 May 1829, and opened between 9 March 1835 and 18 June 1838. The principal engineers were Francis Giles, John Blackmore and William Chapman. At the time the N&C bill was passed, more than a year was to elapse before the Liverpool & Manchester Railway would open, so the N&C had little previous experience to go on. As with other pioneer railways, it was to rely on stagecoach practice in developing the passenger business. The earliest railway carriages were built by established stagecoach builders who mounted a stagecoach on rail wheel. Coaching practice was also adopted at wayside stations. Passengers had purchased handwritten tickets at a Coaching Inn, and boarded the stagecoach from ground level, and the earliest wayside railway

stations comprised a booking hall and a levelled area from which passengers could climb into the coach. At larger stations, refreshments were available, but this would not be the case at smaller places. Many, perhaps all, the original stations on the Newcastle & Carlisle Railway were by Benjamin Green, the son of John Green (1787-1852), a contractor and engineer. After he showed early promise, Benjamin was sent for architectural training in London. On his return, he worked with his father and independently. As with the Stephensons, it is difficult to separate the work of the two Greens, though in general, Benjamin handled architectural work whilst John handled the engineering side, such as bridges. Wetheral station is probably by Benjamin, who died in 1858, only six years after his father. The original two story building in Ashlar-dressed stone with a slate roof was set back from the track, as with a coaching inn, and a ground level boarding area was provided. A later extension in sandstone took the building almost up to the track, and an iron and glass canopy was added at some stage. The Newcastle & Carlisle, although a pioneer railway, was a cross-country route, so did not enjoy the same mushroom growth of traffic that was experienced on the trunk routes from London, so several original stations survived into modern times.

Opposite bottom: The N&C was absorbed into the North Eastern Railway in 1862. The early use of ground level boarding soon gave way to conventional platforms, but rather than replace the existing buildings, they were left undisturbed, passengers booking tickets at the old buildings and then going on to the platform. A public right of way also crossed the station, and a footbridge of standard North Eastern Railway design was added. Wetheral station was closed on 2 January 1967, although trains continued to run on the Newcastle & Carlisle route, but the station reopened following local agitation in 1981. In January 2006, fears that the station could be closed surfaced due to a controversial document leaked from the Strategic Rail Authority, suggesting the closure of rural stations attracting fewer than 100 passengers a day. With only seven trains a day calling at Wetheral, Carlisle Council protested strongly, pointing out that whilst someone could in theory catch the train to work in Carlisle in the morning if they left work at 5.30pm, the next available service calling at Wetheral was not until 9.20pm. Such a service pattern was unlikely to secure the magic 100 passengers a day. We are looking towards Newcastle in September 2006.

Below: The London & Birmingham Railway was not the first railway to enter the capital, but it was the first trunk line to serve London, and with its completion in 1838, rail travel, instead of being something that happened in far away places, now connected London with the Midlands, and this was important. George & Robert Stephenson were engaged as engineers to the L&B in September 1830, but parliamentary approval was not secured until 1833 for a line to commence at Camden in North London, later revised to Euston, and to terminate on the east side of Birmingham. The L&B commissioned Philip Hardwick to create a triumphal arch to herald its entry into London. This was the legendary Doric arch, and its destruction at the start of the 1960s was probably the most outrageous piece of official vandalism in the twentieth century. His grandfather, Thomas Hardwick, Snr, had started the family on the road to fame and fortune in 1760, when he became master mason to Robert and John Adam. His son, Thomas, Jnr, (1752-1829) became an architect & surveyor to St Bartholomew's hospital. Philip Hardwick, (1792-1870) trained under his father, and after the defeat of Napoleon, did the fashionable European tour, studying French and Italian architecture between 1815 and 1819. He took over from his father as surveyor to Barts, and a series of prestigious commissions flowed in. By the 1830s, he was one of the foremost architects in Britain. His European tour had introduced Hardwick to the glories of classical architecture, and 'Propylaeum' or Doric Arch at Euston marked the triumphal entrance to the great way to the north. The L&B board wanted a comparable statement of pride and power in Birmingham. The result was Curzon St station. Unlike the Doric arch, the Curzon St arch was the frontage to the station offices. Rather than repeat the Doric theme with moulded columns, Hardwick opted for Ionic capitals.

Below: Trains started running between Curzon St and Rugby on 9 April 1838, delays in completing Kilsby tunnel precluding through services for some months. The Grand Junction Railway, which had reached the outskirts of Birmingham with a temporary terminus at Duddeston, joined the L&B with their own station on Curzon St in January 1839. In 1846, the L&B and GJR became part of the London & North Western Railway. Curzon St, which comprised two terminal stations side by side, was seen as a bar to through services, and a through station closer to the city centre was sought. Eight years were to elapse, but on 1 June 1854, LNWR passenger services were transferred to New St, Midland Railway trains following a few weeks later. Curzon St now became a goods depot, and Hardwick's magnificent terminal station lingered on, a curious appendage to a major goods depot. Despite being on a curved site with access lines that were too short to accommodate a full-length freight as train lengths increased, Curzon St survived as a goods depot until 1966. At that stage, it looked as if that luck was about to run out. Having destroyed the Doric arch and Great Hall, British Rail saw no reason to save Curzon St, and with the depot due to close to freight in 1966, the end seemed close. I recall visiting it on a grim wet winter's afternoon that was too dark for photography, and wondering if I would see this remarkable structure again. Happily Birmingham City Council stepped in, and acquired the building from BR. Although freight services had ended, part of the depot was retained for engineering use, part as a Royal Mail distribution centre, for parcels traffic and the residue for cement. We see Curzon St yard on 3 July 1976, the seldom-photographed rail

elevation of the Hardwick building appearing in the middle distance. Virtually all the railway infrastructure seen in this view has vanished since 1976.

Opposite top: Although the L&B had grandiose ideas for its termini, it was parsimonious over wayside stations, and between Coventry and Birmingham, there was just one intermediate station in 1838. The line crossed a number of minor roads on the level, and small cottages had been provided for the gatekeepers. One such crossing was Allesley Gate, and on 19 May 1847, the traffic sub-committee of the LNWR, into which the L&B had been merged the previous year, agreed that a few local trains might call at Allesley Gate. Facilities were scant, and in January 1848, the stations committee noted that a new station was required to meet the wishes of the inhabitants. It looked as if a new station was likely, but by 1850, the LNWR was less generous, rejecting the idea of a new station, so the crossing-keeper's house of 1838 had to suffice. On 1 September 1863, Allesley Gate was renamed Allesley Lane, but was further revised to Tile Hill on 1 April 1864. For the next century, the crossing-keeper's house functioned as the station building, but electrification in the sixties finally prompted BR to do something. We are looking from the Down platform towards Coventry on 19 March 1966. The LNWR overhung signal box is on the left, and is located on the Birmingham side of the level crossing. Immediately beyond the gates is what is left of the original station, and beyond that, the old down platform. The near portion is low, only the far section having been raised. On the right is a replacement BR signal box. This was required as the working floor of

the old overhung LNWR box would come perilously close to the 25kV overhead, and because the original up platform on the Coventry side of the level crossing was to be replaced by a new platform on the Birmingham side, ending the use of staggered platforms at Tile Hill after many years. The box stood in the way of the access to the new up platform. Control of the signals would actually be transferred to Coventry Power Signal Box, Tile Hill acting as a crossing keepers box with 'slots' on the running signals to protect the gates when they were closed against the railway.

Opposite bottom: Sadly, we did not hear of the imminent demolition of Tile Hill until work had started, but this portrait of what was left of the building on 19 March 1966 is full of interest, and a bizarre contrast with the opulence of Curzon St just a few miles away. The crossing-keeper's cottage has gone, to make way for the overhead mast in the foreground, but the booking clerk's office and booking corridor have survived for a few weeks longer. I have said 'corridor', as the facilities at Tile Hill could in no way be called a booking hall, as they consisted of a narrow passage open to the breezes, and which was punctuated on the far wall by a ticket window. The clerk's office was separated from the cottage by this corridor, which was at right angles to the track. Passengers entered the station from a tiny road forecourt, on the far side of the building. In the corridor, they bought their tickets at the window, and then walked out of the corridor. Nothing separated them from the track and fast moving trains, other than a post and rail wooden fence that ran along the side of the cottage and led to the foot of the platform

ramp. I can testify from personal experience that leaving the building just as a fast moving express roared by just a few inches from your right elbow was startling. Passenger facilities on the up platform included a Ladies waiting room, which was a standard LNWR hut (For more details see under Morcott) and a Gents convenience further along the platform. As a station, it was basic, but a remarkable survivor from the dawn of railway history on Britain's premier main line! Today the scene is unrecognisable as the LNWR signal box, the level crossing, the old up platform and the BR 1966 box have all been swept away in a series of upgrades.

Above: Although the Stockton & Darlington Railway predated the Liverpool & Manchester by five years, it was envisaged as a coal railway, and passengers were an afterthought. Unlike freight, which was moved by steam, passengers were conveyed in four-wheeled horse-drawn coaches, which followed road practice by stopping where convenient. Indeed the S&D could be called the first tramway as well as the first freight railway. Passenger services were franchised out until 1833, when the company decided that franchising was a mistake, due to the divided responsibility it created, and the company took over, and started running steam hauled passenger services. The result was a marked improvement in efficiency, but necessitated proper stations. At Darlington, part of the freight area was used until 1842, when Darlington North Road station was constructed on the west side of North Road. It comprised a long colonnaded Georgian frontage with a central two-story block flanked by single story extensions. A large trainshed on the far side of the building covered the tracks, and this can be seen beyond the building. Unlike Curzon St, Darlington North Road is still served by trains on the Bishop Auckland branch, but primarily functions as a museum, housing S&DR *Locomotion No 1*. North Road is not as grand as Hardwick's Euston, or Curzon St, but with its museum and rail use, it has been conserved in an appropriate manner to the credit of all concerned.

Opposite top: Great Chesterford, ten miles south of Cambridge, is on the Eastern Counties, later the Great Eastern line from London to Cambridge. The station, which opened on 30 July 1845, is in classical style, following the precedent set by the Liverpool & Manchester, London & Birmingham and the S&D at Darlington North Road. It is a two story rectangular structure, with a continuous shallow canopy projecting out above the ground floor windows on all four sides. The canopy, which does not extend the full width of the platform, is supported by a profusion of wooden struts. Taken with the pronounced cornice at roof level, they mellow a severe appearance into a handsome building at low cost. Great Chesterford station used to be attributed to Sancton Wood, but contemporary sources list Francis Thompson as architect for Audley End, Great Chesterford and Cambridge, and it is now generally accepted to be his work. Thompson is better known for his work on the North Midland Railway and on the Chester & Holyhead, but was born in East Anglia, at Woodbridge, Suffolk, in 1808, his father being a prominent butcher. Thompson married Anna Maria Watson in 1830, and emigrated to Canada. Had personal tragedy not struck the family, with the death of his wife, Thompson might have created stations in Canada, but he returned to England about 1838. He started working for the North Midland Railway at the then remarkable salary of £1,103 per annum, creating Jacobean, Classical and Italianate buildings and also the celebrated Tri-Junct station at Derby. Thompson later worked for the Chester & Holyhead Railway in 1846–50, but seems to have designed stations for the Eastern Counties Railway c1845, his ECR and C&H buildings having many similarities. Thompson seems to have done little architectural work after 1850, although he survived until 1895. A hallmark of Thompson's work was perfect symmetry, which explains his liking for a continuous awning. At many stations, though not at Great Chesterford, the building was centrally placed on the platform. The blocks on the side of the platform wall are steps so that railwaymen could cross the line easily. With movements now restricted to approved walking routes their use is nowadays forbidden, and many have been removed.

Opposite bottom: I K Brunel combined genius and maverick in equal measure. Although some ideas, such as the atmospheric system or the broad gauge, were to cost his employers dearly, he displayed a touch that few engineers have equalled. The viaducts and stations he built for the Great Western Railway and its associated companies included some of the masterpieces of the railway age. Culham, between Didcot and Oxford, is from 1845, and is the oldest surviving Brunellian wayside station. After the initial classical period in the 1830s and early 1840s, when Doric or Ionic colonnades, and the glories of Ancient Greece and Rome were incorporated into the new railway temples, Tudor and Jacobean styles found favour. The term Tudor refers to the Tudor Kings, the most celebrated being Henry VIII, whilst Jacobean refers to the subsequent Stuart era, embracing James I, Charles I, Charles II and James II. For Culham, Brunel used a Tudor motif, but with his own interpretation, with a continuous flat awning that projects from all four sides. Unlike Thompson, who used timber struts to divide an otherwise plain structure at Great Chesterford, Brunel was dealing with a smaller building at Culham, and sought a lighter appearance, supporting the canopy with attractive cast iron spandrels, and providing a fretted bargeboard. Both men were right in the circumstances, and that is a measure of their skill. These Brunellian wayside stations were a marked improvement on early wayside stations such as Wetheral or Tile Hill, but were not the riot of extravagance that was to cost shareholders dear elsewhere. Culham was in local brick, with stone quoins and footings, and is the last survivor from a group of historic structures. We see the platform face, with its projecting bay window on 27 July 1989. In later buildings, Brunel replaced the flat awning with a hipped roof that extended outwards to form a canopy, and an Italianate style supplanted the Tudor theme.

Below: Success prompted a railway boom that peaked in the Railway Mania of 1845–46, when thousands of miles of line were proposed. The London & Birmingham, under George Glyn, was prudent, but aware of the vulnerability of its main line to rivals, and protected itself by throwing off strategic branches that would also access new territory. The 47 mile Blisworth & Peterborough branch, which was authorised in 1843, was to run north-east, protecting the L&B from that direction, and creating a possible route to York and the east coast. Unlike the main line, which had been costly, earthworks were kept to a minimum, and if possible roads were crossed on the level. It was completed as a single line when opened to passenger traffic throughout on 2 June 1845, but preparations were in hand to double it. Although wishing to building the line cheaply, the L&B employed John William Livock as architect. Livock, who was born in 1814, seems to have worked from 1836 to c1875, and produced Tudor or Jacobean stations that were at variance with the strict economy in force. Oundle gained a vast Tudor mansion in ashlar, or dressed stone, a surprising extravagance for a town that even a century after the railway came, had a population of just 3,100 people. Wansford, where the line crossed the old Great North Road on the level, was a few miles to the north. For less than 400 people, Livock created a majestic Jacobean manor house, with the curly gables that distinguish the Jacobean style from the straight edged Tudor gables, the contractor being John Thompson. In 1867, the Stamford & Essendine Railway, which was worked for most of its life by the GNR, built a short branch to Wansford, and after a spell when S&E trains terminated in the fields short of the LNWR station owing to a disagreement, Stamford services used Wansford until they were withdrawn by the LNER in 1929. In 1879, the LNWR built a link from its Rugby & Stamford line at Seaton to the Northampton & Peterborough at Yarwell Junction. Wansford was closed to passengers on 1 July 1957, the

Northampton and Rugby services ending by 1966. A canopy was added later, its position being indicated by the lack of weathering on the stonework on the ground floor, but this was removed after the station closed to passengers. The removal of a canopy is often detrimental, but here it helps, as it restores Livock's concept. The buildings were sold to a haulage company, but Wansford became part of the Nene Valley Railway, which hopes to incorporate them in its railway at some stage. We see the station in June 1966, the shortness of the platform and the size of the building being apparent.

Opposite top: An old rhyme goes that, 'Great Fleas have Little Fleas, and Little Fleas have Smaller Fleas'. That certainly applies to the line from Ipswich to Bury. The decision by the Eastern Counties Railway not to extend from Colchester to Ipswich prompted some ECR directors to form the Eastern Union Railway, to build this section. Meanwhile the lure of Bury St Edmunds proved irresistible, so the Ipswich & Bury Railway was formed, gaining parliamentary approval on 21 July 1845. Peter Schuyler Bruff, (1812–1900), formerly of the ECR, and engineer to the EUR, was also engineer to the I&BR, the contractor being Thomas Brassey. Given the strong Ipswich connections of both companies, a local Ipswich man, Frederick Barnes, was appointed architect. He was born at Hackney in 1814, and was educated at Christ's Hospital School before training under Sidney Smirke. Barnes designed stations at Clayden, Needham, Stowmarket, and Elmswell. The contractor, Revett, commenced work at Stowmarket on 29th October 1846. Of the many painful choices in this book, selecting one station at the expense of another, the decision as to which of Barnes' stations to include has been one of the hardest, as they were all masterpieces. As with Livock, on the Blisworth & Peterborough line, Barnes used Tudor at some stations, and Jacobean elsewhere. Stowmarket, which was completed in 1849, and is seen in May 1990, is in a mellow red brick to exceptionally high

standards, and with its curly gables, is in Jacobean style. The building comprises a central entrance, with end gables pierced by louvered ventilators, and a gable facing the forecourt with a blind window. Single story wings lead to two story blocks with an octagonal tower at the corner. The ECR, EUR and I&B were absorbed into the Great Eastern Railway, which possessed an unusually high proportion of outstanding stations in Suffolk.

Opposite bottom: Until the start of the 1920s, the whole of Ireland was a part of the United Kingdom, but a referendum in the South opted for independence, Southern Ireland becoming the Irish Free State and later Eire. Railway development until the 1920s was similar to England, and whilst the LNWR, the Midland and the GWR had a stake in Ireland, most of the Irish railways were separate companies. The largest was the Great Southern & Western Railway, which ran south west from Dublin to Cork. The GSWR obtained powers in 1844 to build a line through Carlow, which is roughly midway between Dublin and Waterford, the section from Cherryville Junction on the GSWR main line to Carlow opening on 4 August 1846, the line being extended south to Bagenalstown on 24 July 1848. Sir John Benjamin MacNeill, who was born near Dundalk in 1793, became one of Thomas Telford's assistants during the road building era at the close of the Napoleonic wars in 1815. MacNeill set up as an engineer in 1834, and was responsible for the Dublin-Drogheda section of what later became the Great Northern Railway (Ireland) and the Kildare section of the GSWR, being knighted for his work in 1844. During this time, he was also Professor of Civil Engineering at Dublin University, and in 1846 was responsible for designing Carlow Railway station. The station is unusual in that it combines crow stepped and curved Jacobean gables in the single story pavilions at each end of the main building with three straight edged Tudor gables in the central section.

Above: The extension from Carlow to Bagenalstown was not opened until 24 July 1848, but this seems a logical place to explore the next station south from Carlow, as it reveals very different architectural styles. Bagenalstown, now known as Muine Bheag, derives its name from Walter Bagenal, who founded the town in the 18th century. His vision, which was not to be fulfilled, was based on Versailles, the palace of Louis XIV, and fine streets and classical buildings, and he constructed an imposing courthouse based on the Parthenon. When the railway reached Bagenalstown, one of Ireland's foremost architects, William Deane Butler, who trained under Henry Aaron Baker at the Dublin Society Schools, was commissioned to design a suitable station. In deference to the style set by Walter Bagenal, Butler created an imposing Neo-classical block, which we see in this view, as Irish Rail General Motors Bo-Bo No 079 enters the station with a down train from Dublin to Waterford. Butler, who died in 1857, was responsible for some of Ireland's finest buildings, including the Dublin Amiens St terminus and headquarters of the Great Northern Railway (Ireland), which, with its classic Campanile Tower, is one of the finest Italianate buildings in Ireland.

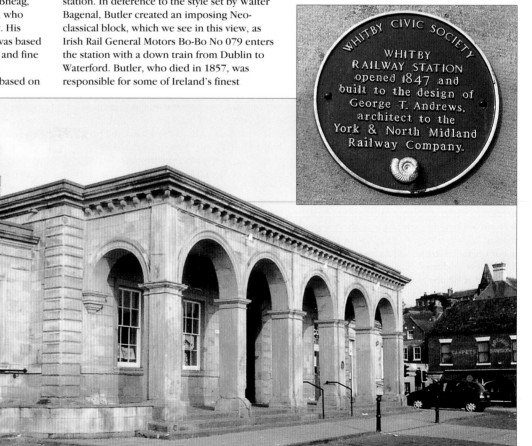

Opposite bottom: George Hudson, the 'Railway King' rose to fame during the railway mania, and crashed into obscurity even more rapidly, but during his meteoric career, he added substantially to the railway network. Many of his stations have long gone, but some fascinating examples survive in East Yorkshire. George Townsend Andrews, who was an architect, builder, and High Sheriff of York, was a close friend of Hudson, and in a position to do him many favours in his official capacity, which the Railway King reciprocated by giving Andrews a great deal of work. Although Andrews was chosen because of his ability to arrange things for Hudson, and after Hudson's fall, vanished from railway work, though he did not die until 1855, he was a talented, even a brilliant architect.Hudson's association with Andrews included Whitby, a town for which he had a sentimental attachment, and which he saw as a potential boom town, investing heavily in developments in the area. After Hudson's York & North Midland Railway acquired the horse-worked Whitby & Pickering Railway in 1845, a major upgrade started, and Andrews emerged as architect. Andrews' characteristic hipped roof trainshed at Whitby has long vanished, but Whitby station was additionally graced with a five arched porte cochere in dressed stone, with a row of equally spaced dentils, or small rectangular stone blocks beneath the projecting cornice. Happily, this grade 2 listed structure survives. Apart from his railway work for Hudson, George Townsend Andrews was responsible for a number of excellent churches in the North East, and designed the de Grey Rooms in York in 1841, which hosted the Yorkshire Hussars Regiment Annual ball, and took their name from the regiment's colonel, Earl de Grey. The rooms were also used for public concerts, balls, meetings and

entertainment. Although we have only reached 1847, a pattern is emerging, with important stations being entrusted to leading architects such as Hardwick, Thompson or Andrews.

Above: The Liverpool & Manchester Railway adopted an unglazed wooden trainshed at Crown St in 1830, and the idea of a trainshed for quite small towns survived until the early 1850s. Many of Hudson's early stations followed this plan, but as is the case elsewhere, subsequent enlargements have swept most of them away. The Andrews' trainshed at Beverley was illustrated in 'Railway Infrastructure'. In this volume, I have selected his trainshed at Filey, which dates from 1846. This iron-trussed hipped roof represents a dramatic advance on the gloomy and claustrophobic wooden structure at Crown St. The roof is higher than Crown St, and includes a longitudinal central clerestory, to provide a glazed area.

Below: Pillars with ornate flared capitals were provided at each end of the trainshed walls, and these carried an astonishing girder that at first sight appears to have little structural strength. Unlike the more common and better understood lattice girder with its diagonal bracing, the girders that Andrews used at Filey consist of top and bottom members connected by closely spaced verticals, but a closer inspection reveals that Andrews has created a double Bowstring Girder, one member being rivetted to the bottom chord at the pillars and to the top chord at the centre, whilst the second bowstring is inverted. The deceptive painting scheme, with the verticals in red, but the horizontals and curved bowstrings in black, makes it even more confusing, but this double bowstring, although lightly built, possesses considerable strength, and suggests that Andrews was an ingenious structural engineer as well as a talented architect.

Opposite top: The line from the North Kent coast near Minster and Ramsgate to Dover was not a continuous route, but due to the contorted railway politics of the area. The South Eastern Railway opened from Minster to Deal on 1 July 1847, whilst the section from Deal to Buckland Junction, near Dover, was jointly built by the SER and the London, Chatham & Dover Railway, and opened in 1881. Sandwich, which is between Minster and Deal, was one of the five Cinque Ports established by Royal Charter in 1155. With its narrow streets, Sandwich is one of the most complete medieval towns in England, with a high concentration of listed buildings. This includes the station, to a Neo-Classical design in dark blue brick with stone mouldings, including a heavy cornice. The main building of 1847 would have been built under the direction of P W Barlow who had succeeded William Cubitt as Chief Engineer to the SER in 1844, and served in this role until 1851. The architect is unknown. Samuel Beazley, who did a lot of work for the SER at this time, including Canterbury West, the Lord Warden Hotel in Dover, Erith, Gravesend Central, and Dartford, is possible, as the SER would have been likely to have employed an architect they were familiar with for a station serving one of the Cinque Ports, but that is surmise. This view, from July 1973, shows the building in good condition. Sadly it was in poor state with the upper floor windows boarded up by 2004.

Opposite bottom: We encountered Francis Thompson at Great Chesterford on the Eastern Counties Railway, Thompson's next challenge was the Chester & Holyhead Railway, which was to be the great artery between London and Dublin, then a part of the United Kingdom. This contract commenced with Chester, a superb station, and stretched across Wales and into Anglesey. The earlier stations were excellent, but by the time the C&H had constructed the Britannia bridge across the Menai straits, money had run out, and the remaining stations were meagre, making the contrast with Flint and stations to the east even more pronounced. The general theme was Italianate with shallow hipped roofs, flared chimney stacks and overhanging eaves. Many of the stations, such as Fflint, originally spelled Flint, had an armorial device on the road frontage. On the road elevation, two projecting wings flanked the two-story central section, with a pair of small single story pavilions beyond them, creating an interesting frontage. The contract for constructing Flint station went to Thomas Hughes at £4,401.

Above: From the platform, the treatment was different. The main frontage was flush, with the pavilions projecting beyond the building to provide support for a modest canopy. Given Thompson's love of symmetry, the single extension to the near pavilion with its sloping roof is a later addition that does nothing for the lines of this superb structure. Even the most cursory examination reveals a wealth of detail, the window surrounds being particularly fine. Construction of a railway to serve Holyhead had taken a leap forward after the 1838 report of a

government commission that had been set up to consider railway development in Ireland, but had also covered rail communication to and from Ireland. Later reports selected Holyhead as the best Packet port, due to the short sea crossing, and backed a connecting railway along the North Wales coast. The first short section of the Chester & Holyhead Railway at Chester opened in 1846. The next section, along the North Wales coast to Bangor, which included Flint, following on 1 May 1848, and the Anglesey section a few months later. Although worked by the LNWR, the C&H was not absorbed into the North Western until 1859. Unlike the coast towns such as Rhyl, Colwyn Bay and Llandudno, which became popular seaside resorts, and required new stations to cope with the heavy traffic, Flint did not see the same growth, and although its population of 14,257 people in 1951 was close to the 16,712 population of Llandudno, it did not see the massive summer traffic. The town was large enough to retain its station unlike some of the other North Wales stations, but quiet enough not to require replacement.

Below: The main building on the down platform was set off by a single story waiting room and shelter on the up platform. Although this did not appear until 1883 when the station was rebuilt, it was not a standard LNWR wooden shelter, but followed the Italianate theme, with prominent flared chimney stacks and a shallow roof. As at Great Chesterford, the canopy was supported by a profusion of wooden struts that had echoes of Thompson's work at Great Chesterford. The footbridge is a standard LNWR design that appeared at the start of the 1890s, and became widespread over the next thirty years. The bulbous outriggers on the horizontal span characterised the Crewe designed bridges, and provided a measure of triangulation and stiffening to the lightweight lattice girders that gave the bridge its structural strength. Built from mass produced components, these bridges could be assembled in various ways.

Above: Today, we are used to separate up and down platforms on double track lines, but in the pioneering days of railways, everything was new, and there were few inevitable answers. Some engineers advocated one long platform at which all trains would arrive or depart via suitable connections. The early stations at Reading, Gloucester and Cambridge followed this pattern, Cambridge retaining this concept. However, there was one station where it was carried to an extraordinary conclusion. This was Limerick Junction, which is located in County Tipperary, and is just over 2 miles from Tipperary, but is over 20 miles from Limerick City. The honour of discovering Limerick

Junction goes to the Waterford & Limerick Railway, which opened from Limerick City to Tipperary in the late spring of 1848. Two months later, the Great Southern & Western Railway main line from Dublin to Cork arrived from the north, crossing the W&L at right angles. The W&L had not bothered to provide a station at Limerick Junction, as there was nothing to serve until the GSWR arrived. The GSWR line extended south to Mallow on 19 March 1849, and a working practice, that has in essence survived for over a century and a half, evolved. A long Island platform, which was a short distance south of the square crossing with the W&L, and capable of holding two main line

trains, was built to one side of the GSWR main line. Trailing points were provided from the Dublin and Cork lines into this platform, and a train from Dublin overshot the station and then reversed into the northern portion of the main platform No 1. A train from Cork also overshot the station, and reversed into the southern half of the platform, No 3. The two engines were then facing one another only a few yards apart. When the trains were ready to depart they pulled away to continue their journey. In this view we are looking from Limerick Junction South Signal box towards the platform on 15 July 1996. A track diagram appears on page 26.

Opposite bottom: We are looking from the southbound part of the platform towards Cork on 15 July 1996. When Limerick junction opened, and for well over 100 years, all Dublin to Cork trains had to run past this platform and then reverse in, but a facing connection from the down main line to the Cork platform was laid in, so that Dublin-Cork expresses could arrive in the platform normally. They will depart over the diamond crossing in the middle distance, and run via a ladder junction to reach the down main line which is the third track. Up expresses also had to pass the station and then set back over the points in the foreground into the Dublin portion of this long platform, but a facing connection was laid in permitting them to enter the platform normally. Limerick Junction South Signal box is visible in the distance. The two wagons are standing on a short loop track that permits interchange of freight stock, and once provided access to Limerick Junction loco shed, but by this time provided access to the track machine depot. The square shunt signal is an Irish development of the common disc signal.

Right: At the north end of the station, the Limerick City to Waterford line of the former Waterford, Limerick & Western Railway crossed the GSWR main line almost at right angles. The driver of Irish Rail General Motors Bo-Bo No 190 leans out of his cab to collect the single line miniature electric train staff for the Limerick Junction North SB to Tipperary section in July 1996. This is a through train from Limerick City to Waterford, and in the past the driver would also hand over a train staff for the single line section he had just left, from Dromkeen to Limerick Junction North Signal box, but this section is now operated by CTC, or Centralised Traffic Control from the signalling centre at Dublin Connolly. No 190 is one of a dozen members of the 181 class of 1966. They were developed from the earlier 141 class, and came from the legendary La Grange, Illinois, plant of General Motors.

Below: Whilst main line trains can now reach the platform without reversal, the old method of reversal still applies on the Waterford-Limerick section. In this view we are looking from the northern end of the W&L platform. Bo-Bo No 153 has arrived from Waterford and crossed over the square junction (A on the plan) seen in our previous view and stopped beyond the points (B) from the W&L into the Junction platform. It has then propelled its train backwards via the connecting curve into Platform No 2 where it is waiting until the train from Limerick City has arrived. The Limerick City-Limerick Junction-Waterford train, which is hauled by No 189, is on the third line. It has approached the station on the same chord as the train from Waterford, but rather than entering the occupied platform No 2, is on the third track (C). This goes round the back of the station, passing over the station approach drive by a level crossing, (D) and will stop south of the station (E). It will then reverse into the Waterford bay, platform No 4, which is the far side of the station buildings.

Limerick Junction

To Limerick City

B

D LC FB

E

C

North
S B

4

2

3

1

A

To
Cork

Limerick Junction
South Signal Box

To
Dublin

Some Sidings omitted
for clarity

To Waterford

Opposite top: Irish Rail No 189 has brought its train into the bay platform, which is in the shadow of the station canopy. The train has completed the necessary station duties, and the driver has set forward out of the platform into the dead-end headshunt at the south end of the station. The points are then changed to permit him to propel his train over the pedestrian level crossing and all the way round the chord to the WLW main line. The North box will reset the route for Waterford, and the train will finally depart forward, crossing the Dublin–Cork line at the square junction, the driver picking up the Limerick Junction–Tipperary electric train staff as he does so. One of the station employees stands by the hand worked barriers on the pedestrian level crossing. When train movements take place over the crossing, pedestrians can use the footbridge, but other than for a couple of youngsters using it as a vantage point to watch the antics of the trains, I did not see many people using it. Although working methods that necessitate the Waterford-Limerick trains entering the platform in reverse seem bizarre, and add a good deal to the journey time, the positive side of the curious arrangements at Limerick Junction is that passengers changing trains do not need to change platforms via a footbridge or subway. The system can only survive because of the relatively infrequent train service provided. Had traffic in Ireland grown as it had in England, the delays occasioned by such working practices would have led to its elimination, as was the case at Reading more than a century ago.

Although diesel traction has long replaced steam at Limerick Junction, the station provides a living example of working practices that were tried out at the dawn of railways, and discarded on the busier lines in England.

Opposite bottom: To assist in understanding train movements to and from the Waterford & Limerick bays, I have included this track plan of Limerick Junction. Some sidings at the Cork end of the station and at the former loco shed are omitted for clarity, but train movements can be followed by means of the diagram and explanatory letters which also appear in the text relating to some of the other views. Perhaps I may leave this description of a fascinating station with a comment made to me by one of the signalmen who worked it, 'The man who designed this station was a genius'. Few people would agree with him, but for passengers changing trains, it is convenient, even though the delay may be less welcome, and with the limited train service that can be justified on the Waterford section, the delays are not an insuperable problem.

Below: Sir John Fowler (1817-1898), whose distinguished career covered over half a century, was the engineer for the Scunthorpe and Grimsby section of the Manchester, Sheffield & Lincolnshire Railway. Fowler had been born at Derby, and worked under J U Rastrick on the London & Brighton, and later became resident engineer of the Stockton & Hartlepool Railway. Setting up as a consulting engineer in 1844, he engineered several lines that later became a part of the MS&L. His later career included the Metropolitan Railway and the Forth Bridge, two of the most challenging engineering feats of the nineteenth century. By the 1840s, civil engineers were used to demands for special stations to serve the nobility, and with the line passing close to the entrance to Brocklesby Park, the seat of the Earl of Yarborough, it was not surprising that something special was called for at Brocklesby, as the Earl, apart from being the landowner, also happened to be the chairman of the MS&LR ! The Neo-Jacobean station that was opened on 1 November 1848 was a riot of curly gables that distinguished the Jacobean style from the plainer Tudor style. Unlike many stations of this period that later received large canopies that jarred with their Tudor or Jacobean image, the canopies at Brocklesby were modest, as this view from 4 August 1989 reveals. A private waiting room was provided for the Earl and his family. The magnificent new station received a royal visitor the following year. Prince Albert, the Prince Consort, had agreed to lay the foundation stone of the new dock at Grimsby, and on 17 April 1849 arrived at Brocklesby to stay overnight with the Earl of Yarborough before continuing on to Grimsby the following morning. The engine crew on that trip was distinguished, as it comprised John Fowler, the MSL engineer, and Richard Peacock, the youthful Locomotive Superintendent who was shortly to found Beyer Peacock & Co, one of the legendary locomotive manufacturers.

Above: Gobowen is a small community located in Shropshire close to the Welsh border, and is on the Shrewsbury & Chester Railway, later part of the GWR. The northern section of the S&C between Ruabon and Saltney Junction just outside Chester opened to passengers on 4 November 1846, and the southern section between Ruabon and Shrewsbury on 14 October 1848. Gobowen station, which is on the southern part of the S&C, became a junction a few months later, when a short branch to Oswestry was opened to passengers on 23 December 1848. The main buildings on the down platform are probably the finest surviving example of Florentine Italianate architecture in the United Kingdom. The Oswestry line lost passenger services as a result of the Beeching cuts, and Gobowen fell on evil times, the station buildings being neglected. Thankfully, their historic importance was recognised in time, and restoration work by

British Rail commenced on 29 February 1988, with financial support from English Estates, Oswestry Borough Council, the Railway Heritage Trust and Shropshire County Council. I considered whether to illustrate the station before, during, or after restoration, but opted for a view when the coal concentration depot was still in operation, and showing the station in its latter-day BR condition before restoration began. There are many delightful touches, as for example the curved end bay, with its ecclesiastical connotations, or the manner in which round-headed windows are used singly, in couplets, or as triplets in the Florentine tower. The crude removal of a heavy porch that was added at some time above the entrance has not helped the overall appearance. The marks to the stucco, and the damage to the moulding above the door, are all too apparent.

Opposite bottom: On the up platform, facilities include a single story lodge at ground level, and a further building on the up platform, the left hand structure probably being contemporary with the main building. When this view was taken in May 1989, restoration work was well under way, and the superb GWR 'Running-In Board' had been resurrected. Gobowen is unusual as the station canopies are free standing, i.e. entirely separate from the station buildings, although both buildings had short canopies projecting over the platforms as well. Gobowen now forms the boundary between Railtrack North West Territory and Railtrack Western Territory.

Above right: We are looking towards Chester c1980. The bay platform on the down side is used as a part of the coal concentration depot. A hopper discharge facility was provided on the line next to the bay, and HBA hoppers are positioned on both lines. The coal was moved via the inclined conveyor to the left of the HBA to a funnel hopper, and from there to the various stacking hoppers by means of a movable conveyor that could be swung round in an arc. The Up bay is occupied by CCE track machines, whilst the up sidings were also in use at this time, providing further operational interest. The Oswestry line, although closed to passengers, had been retained for stone out of Nantmawr Quarry.

Below: Our final view is looking south, with the now demolished Gobowen South Signal Box still surrounded by a maze of tracks and with a class 37 at the head of a northbound freight in the vicinity of the box. 356 yards separated the two boxes, the North box being the smaller and controlling the level crossing, whilst the South

box controlled the connections to the bay platforms, the yard and the Oswestry branch. In the days of unfitted freight trains, great care had to be taken approaching Gobowen South from Oswestry and where loads of 35 or more wagons were being worked, enginemen would come to a stand near Gobowen South Distant signal to check whether the Home signal from the branch to the main line was at danger or clear for them. The reason this was necessary was that distant signals from branch lines were commonly fixed at danger, so the driver had no advance warning as to the position of the home signal, and had to assume the most restrictive situation. Stone traffic from the quarries ended in 1988, after which the branch was mothballed, although a weed killing special ran as late as 1993.

Above: Ormskirk, on the northern outskirts of Merseyside, was on the Liverpool, Ormskirk & Preston Railway, later a part of the Lancashire & Yorkshire Railway. The line ran from a junction with the North Union Railway south of Preston to join the Liverpool & Bury Railway at Walton-on-the-Hill, and opened on 2 April 1849, an 1848 target date proving over optimistic. Joseph Locke and John Errington were joint chief engineers. The original Neo-classical stone station buildings were on the north side of the line, with a two bay hipped roof, mullioned windows, i.e. the window divided by stone verticals, and a neat row of projecting blocks or dentils beneath the cornice just below roof level. At a later date, a new red brick building was provided on the opposite side of the line. The Liverpool, Ormskirk & Preston was an important through route between Liverpool and north-east Lancashire until 1969, when through services were withdrawn. Apart from through trains, the service pattern fell into two parts. South of Ormskirk, the line carried a heavy suburban service to and from Liverpool, and had been electrified as far as Ormskirk in 1911, as a part of the LYR electric network radiating out from Liverpool (Exchange) station. North of Ormskirk, the line was rural in character with a less frequent service, and with the abandonment of through services, the track north of Ormskirk was singled. So that the old platform could be taken out of service, the electric line south of Ormskirk station was also singled just short of the station, trains arriving and departing from the former southbound platform line. Back to back buffer stops were installed in the middle of the platform, to prevent trains overrunning and colliding with one another. We are looking towards Preston on 22 June 1989, with BR Merseyside electric set 507009 in the platform.

Left: The LYR buildings on the Up platform were to a totally different style to the original 1849 LO&P stone buildings, but the combination of round headed windows and a projecting bay window made for an attractive result. The way in which the canopy roof line is level and then inclined upwards is unusual, as is the provision of a false front which makes the building look grander than it really is. The platform was originally much lower, the rough cut or rock faced stone in the lower three courses of stonework being original. Brick courses, which are heavily weathered with brake dust and third rail shoe dust, have been added on top of them to increase the height of the platform coping. In January 2006, the West Lancashire Council met with Merseyrail and Merseytravel to discuss proposals to extend the electric service a short distance on to Burscough Junction, and the possibility of reinstating the south curve at Burscough, which connected the LO&P with the Southport line.

HIGH VICTORIAN ELEGANCE
1850–1875

By 1850, the pioneering days were over. The majority of important main lines had been completed although the decade was to commence with the completion of the last section of the Great Northern Main line from King's Cross to Peterborough. The great companies that were to dominate the railway industry had mostly come into existence, and railways were now an established part of life. Although some of the great men who had guided railways in their infancy were still active, amongst them Robert Stephenson and Isambard Kingdom Brunel, a new cast of characters was taking the reins. The emphasis switched from great new lines to filling in the gaps, creating a network of branch lines and in developing and enlarging existing lines and stations.

Right: To the established companies, Edmund Denison's Great Northern Railway was an unwelcome rival, and they sought to block it, but with Denison's determination, a main line was driven from King's Cross to Doncaster and a junction with the NER, creating the East Coast Main Line. The section from Peterborough to London was opened on 7 August 1850. It was a tribute to the engineering skills of the Cubitt family, a remarkable engineering dynasty, who filled a variety of jobs on the GN in its early years. In the immediate environs of London, where early quadrupling resulted in a string of drab timber stations, the urban environment meant that many stations became down-at-heel,

but further north, it was different. A rural environment avoided the grime of the cities, whilst the pleasing buff brick gave a lighter and more welcoming appearance than would have been the case with red brick. Many were by a well-known Lincoln architect, Henry Goddard (1813-1899), including Huntingdon and Sandy. Goddard's brief had been to keep costs down, which he did by omitting ornament as far as possible. Round-headed Italianate windows, and shallow overhanging roofs characterised Goddard's work for the GN. We see the station forecourt at Sandy in February 1976.

Below: The main building, on the down side included a single story booking office and a two

story station house, with a short canopy over the exit to the platform. Attractive gas lamps still offered an old world touch in 1976, whilst the parcel weighing machine under the canopy acts as a further reminder of the traditional railway station. The Eastern Region dark blue station signs and the SANDY totem were commonplace for many years, but are now sought-after collectors' items. The main buildings have survived with little alteration, despite quadrupling in the 1970s, and subsequent electrification. Goddard's GN main line stations have received scant respect from generations of writers. This is a pity as they were competently designed within tight financial guidelines, and provided adequate facilities for passengers.

Opposite top: Sandy became a junction in 1857. A local landowner, Captain Robert Peel, RN, felt that a railway would benefit the community of Potton where he lived when not on duty, and subscribed most of the funds for the railway that opened whilst he was on active service in India. Sadly he died on duty and never saw his railway in operation. In 1860, the Bedford & Cambridge Railway, which was backed by the LNWR, was authorised to extend the cross-country route that already stretched from Oxford to Bletchley on to the second great varsity town. This opened in 1862, and because it utilised the S&P for some distance, crossed over the GN north of Sandy station, and dropped down steeply to a joint station on the east side of the GN main line. The LNWR line was closed to passengers between Bedford and Cambridge on 1 January 1968 and subsequently lifted. We are looking north from the GN signal box at Sandy in February 1976, with the former GN goods yard on the left, a DMU in the Up GN platform and a couple of wagons sitting in the former interchange sidings between the GN and LNW lines. The LNW side of the station has been lifted. Although the GN main line was quadruple track north and south of Sandy, the existence of the LNWR line precluded quadrupling through the station, and this may have been a key factor in the decision to close it, as the line had not been included in the Beeching report. Shortly after this view was taken, quadruple track was extended through the station. The right hand platform was demolished, and quadruple track installed with a new platform on the extreme right.

Opposite bottom: The Up GN line platform, which was swept away during the 1970s remodelling of the station, is the subject of our final view of Sandy. The building, although shared by the LNWR and GN, was a Great Northern structure, and a good match to the main buildings on the down platform. Quadrupling of many sections in steam days, preparations for the introduction of HSTs at the end of the 1970s, and electrification work a decade later, have laid a heavy hand on the 1850s infrastructure. The platform 2 sign, although it looks almost chocolate in colour, is not a Western Region sign, but a heavily weathered dark blue Eastern Region sign, rather than the later Corporate Image white sign. For many years, the GN and LNWR stations, although side by side on the same site, were separately administered, each with their own station master.

Below: The Norman Conquest of 1066 is one of the few dates that is firmly anchored in English history. The Battle of Hastings took place some distance from the modern town of Hastings, and the victorious Normans erected Battle Abbey near the spot. Just under eight hundred years later, the South Eastern Railway extended its Tunbridge Wells branch to Hastings, trains reaching Battle on 1 January 1852, and Hastings on 1 February 1852. In the latter part of the Nineteenth century, the SER was not very highly thought of, its suicidal strife with the London, Chatham & Dover reducing both concerns to penury, but the stations between Tunbridge Wells and Hastings were to a high standard, with Battle being outstanding. The architect was William Tress, and he created a medieval railway station in deference to nearby Battle Abbey and this historic site. Lancet windows that would be at home in a church abound, as does a steeply pitched roof with exposed beams that reinforces the ecclesiastical theme. The main building, on the up platform, is built in rough coursed rubble, a term that sounds derogatory, but actually means small random sized pieces of stone that have not been squared or smoothed off. This is in keeping with the ecclesiastical theme, as are the lancet windows, the steeply pitched roof and the delightful belfry tower. The ground plan even conforms to the medieval theme, with a central hall with cross wings recreating the shape of early ecclesiastical buildings. A neatly fretted out ornamental valance fronts the station canopy, the pattern being common to SER stations in Kent. This canopy was added in the 1880s, and although it detracts from the ecclesiastical theme, it provides much appreciated shelter from the elements for the passenger.

Above: Glendon & Rushton station was on the MR Leicester – Bedford – Hitchin line, a few miles south east of Leicester. When the MR was formed in 1844, it relied on connections with the LNWR at Birmingham, Hampton and Rugby for traffic to and from London. Powers for an independent route to the south under Midland auspices were obtained in 1847, but allowed to lapse. After a proposed merger between the MR and LNWR was vetoed by parliament in 1853, the MR obtained powers for a 63 mile line from Leicester to Market Harborough, Bedford and a junction with the GNR at Hitchin, which would avoid the congestion that had developed on the LNWR main line south of Rugby. The new line was opened to coal traffic on 15 April 1857, to freight on 4 May, and to passengers on 8 May 1857. The Midland was going through a financial crisis at the time, and the board ordered that the line was to cost no more than £15,000 per mile. The stations on the Hitchin extension were designed by C H Driver, and due to the need for economy, the smaller stations were highly standardised and devoid of ornamentation, save for a fretted bargeboard, and diamond or lozenge pattern round-headed window frames in the single story station building. These windows, which used a cast iron frame, simulated leaded lights, in which the individual pieces of glass are supported in a frame of shaped soft lead. The two-story station masters house butted on to the booking office, and in some cases the windows were patterned,

but not all, a distinction that is very obvious in this view of Glendon station taken on 1 October 1971. The station buildings were built using local materials, including red brick, pale yellow-white brick, ironstone, and in the case of Glendon, grey limestone. The combination of the station masters house with the booking office and waiting room in a T shape with a shallow crosspiece had developed early in the railway age for wayside stations, and was to be repeated with variations over many decades, but the Leicester–Hitchin stations were a particularly successful group, despite the cash constraints. Glendon, which closed to passengers in 1960, survives as a Grade II listed building.

Opposite bottom: Robert Sinclair was one of those early railwaymen who could put his hand to almost anything. When the Caledonian Railway was formed in 1845, he became its first locomotive engineer, but also served as General Manager. Realising that the existing locomotive facilities were inadequate, he moved the company works to St Rollox, in the Springburn area of Glasgow, the new works opening in 1856, in which year Sinclair migrated south to join the Eastern Counties Railway as Locomotive Superintendent. In 1862, when the Eastern Counties was merged with other railways to form the Great Eastern Railway, Sinclair took over as Locomotive Superintendent of the enlarged company, serving at Stratford until December 1865. Being locomotive superintendent of two important

railways, general manager of one and founding one of the legendary locomotive works should be sufficient to ensure his place in history, but Sinclair is one of the forgotten men of railway history. This is surprising, as Stratford was sufficiently important to attract no less a figure than Samuel Waite Johnson as Sinclair's successor in 1866, and his successor was William Adams. It may be that Sinclair has receded into obscurity because he was just too late to count as one of the pioneers, and just too early for any of his engines to have survived into living memory. Although his engines have long gone, it is one of the paradoxes of railway life that one important example of his work is still used by thousands of people every day, for Robert Sinclair turned his versatile mind to designing Ipswich station. Although a locomotive engineer and manager, rather than an architect, his design for the 1860 station building is regarded as an outstanding piece of GER Italianate architecture, its roof line being enlivened by a profusion of decorative chimneys with contrasting stringer courses, and three belfry towers. Sadly, these lack the necessary bells to summon train worshippers to the station. One reason why such a large building was required was that the design for Ipswich station harked back to the early days of providing a single platform face to and from which all trains ran. My father seldom ventured in front of the camera, but appears in this view with tripod and camera ready to film any train movements.

Above: Unlike Cambridge, which retains the archaic arrangement of a single long platform face, Ipswich later received a facing platform, with an ornate footbridge connecting the old and new portions of the station, but Sinclair's buildings have endured long after the locomotives of his more celebrated contemporaries have retired to the scrap heap or become museum pieces. Although a modern BR canopy has not helped the look of Sinclair's building, the saw tooth profile canopy on the opposite platform adds distinction to the station. In some ways, Robert Sinclair, locomotive engineer, manager and architect, had the last laugh after all. Sinclair was born in London in 1817, serving his apprenticeship with his uncle, who was one of the partners in Scott, Sinclair & Co of Greenock. He then joined the Liverpool & Manchester Railway, but after a short spell in France, was appointed locomotive engineer to the Glasgow, Paisley & Greenock Railway, soon to become the Caledonian, where he later held the additional post of resident civil engineer. He joined the ECR as locomotive superintendent in 1856, and when Peter Bruff retired as civil engineer in 1857, added these duties to his responsibilities. He died in Italy in 1898. We see the station in May 1990, after 25kV electric working had been introduced to East Anglia. The 361 yard long tunnel that pierces Stoke Hill is visible beyond the station throat.

Opposite top: The Pen-y-Darren tramway, which was the site of Trevithick's pioneering 1804 experiments with locomotives, was in South Wales, but despite this promising start, railway construction lagged in Wales. Except on the north coast and in South Wales, rugged terrain, few people and limited industry offered little to the railway promoter. The early foothold that the LNWR and GWR achieved in the north and south meant that unlike Scotland, where great companies such as the Caledonian or North British grew to equal their southern neighbours in power and prestige, the only Welsh railway of any size was the Cambrian Railways, which was an 1860s amalgamation of a string of impoverished local companies serving mid-Wales. The Cambrian main line tapped the GWR and LNWR at Wrexham, Whitchurch and Buttington, and ran via Welshpool to Dovey Junction, where one line turned south to Aberystwyth, whilst another line ran north, passing Towyn, before reaching Barmouth and Pwllheli. The section northwards from Dovey Junction was authorised in July 1861, and reached a temporary terminus at Llwyngwril on 24 October 1863, Towyn being a little north of Aberdovey. Money was tight, which was why the line was opened in sections, so ornamentation was kept to a minimum. This was also in keeping with the Welsh traditions of thrift, and with the strong chapel ethos in Wales, where the exuberances of High Church Gothic were seen with disfavour. A simple brick building, devoid of ornamentation was economical, and

in accord with national sentiment. The only extravagance was a lean-to shelter carried on transverse beams resting on wooden posts set into the platform, and on simple cream coloured corbels that can still be seen in this 1973 portrait of the station after the removal of the canopy.

Opposite bottom: Goods facilities at Towyn consisted of a timber and felt goods shed, and a long loading bank. Although freight facilities had been withdrawn from most wayside stations in England, and coal concentration depots saw the number of stations handling coal fall dramatically, the poor road network in central Wales, and the long distances resulted in rail freight facilities lingering on long after they had vanished from more populated areas. A loading bank, though often much shorter than this, was common at goods depots, but the discharge of coal on to a raised loading bank was unusual. However, the ramshackle mixture of wooden baulks, old second hand railway sleepers and rusty corrugated iron which separate different grades of coal, and the coal stacks of different merchants, was normal, as is the rusty 16T steel mineral wagon, and the empty coal sacks lying where the dock has been extended at some time. The concreted area in the siding is to make it easier to shovel up the inevitable spillage from the wagon when it is unloaded. There has been a good deal of spillage on the track to the right of the concreted area, and the 'ballast', which is

probably a mixture of old cinder ballast, coal dust and dirt that has been there for decades, is a marked contrast to the stone ballast on the running line.

Above: The Cambrian arrived at Towyn in 1863. Two years later, the narrow gauge Talyllyn Railway was opened to bring slate down from the quarries at Abergynolwyn for shipment to the outside world from a wharf adjoining the main line, giving the TR station the name it still carries today, WHARF. Although passengers were conveyed up and down the valley, this was subsidiary to the slate traffic. The quarries fell on evil times in 1910, and were to close. However, a local businessman, Henry Haydn Jones, who was the prospective parliamentary candidate for the local constituency in a forthcoming election, stepped in. Unlike most politicians, who promise the earth with the taxpayers' money, and quietly forget their promises once they have been elected, Haydn Jones not merely kept his promises, but used his own money to do so. He kept the quarry going until it was worked out in 1946, and the trains continued to run until after his death in 1950. It was just long enough, and thanks to a handful of dedicated enthusiasts led by L T C Rolt, the Talyllyn Railway opened the preservation era in 1951. The slate wharf was very valuable to the infant TRPS in its early days, and was used for deliveries of coal, rails, sleepers, and even Corris Railway Nos 3 and 4.

Below: Richard Moon became chairman of the LNWR in 1861 at the early age of 47, having already been a director for ten years. By North Western standards, the company's finances were at a low ebb, though most railways would have been envious. Moon was not the ruthless skinflint that many writers claim, but a shrewd businessman who recognised that to get the best officers, you paid good salaries, and that reliable service without extravagance was the way forward. Compared to many railways, the LNWR provided excellent service, but under Moon it was to do so without the extravagance that had characterised railway construction in earlier days. Even before becoming chairman, he had considerable influence in this direction, but one of the first lines to be opened, 'in the light of the new Moon', was the LNWR branch from Aston to Sutton Coldfield in 1862. Drawings were prepared for standard wooden buildings with rusticated boarding, and windows in twins or triplets. If a canopy was necessary, as at Erdington, which is seen in 1977, the roof was extended to overhang the platform. Such buildings could be put up quickly and were economical to maintain. The purist might say that they are not Tudor, Jacobean, Domestic Revival or to any particular style, or say that they are railway vernacular, a term intended to mean nondescript, but their purpose was to allow passengers to book tickets, and wait in comfort and warmth in inclement weather. They were the harbingers of modular buildings that were to characterise the LNWR, the LMS and the London Midland Region of BR for over a century.

Opposite top: St Deny's is on the outskirts of Southampton, where the Fareham line, which runs via Netley, diverges from the original London & Southampton main line. When the main line opened in the 1840s, the area did not merit a station, but population growth led to the provision of the first station in this area in 1861. Known as Portwood, it was replaced between 1866 and 1868 when the Netley line was opened, and renamed St Deny's in 1876. It is an example of how an architect's ideas can continue long after his association with a company finished, for it is clearly in the Tite style. Sir William Tite was one of the giants of British architecture in the early part of the nineteenth century, his best-known work being the Royal Exchange building. For the opening of the London & Southampton Railway in 1838–1840, Tite provided classical facades at Nine Elms and Southampton Town, the original termini, and symmetrical two-story hipped-roof buildings for intermediate stations. Aware that many of the L&M stations had been hopelessly inadequate for the traffic within a year or two, the L&S felt it was 'prudent, and ultimately economical, to construct these establishments on the requisite scale at the outset', but were keen not to waste money on excessive ornamentation, so Tite's plain but neat Italianate villas were ideal. Having developed a house style, long before such concepts became fashionable, the London & South Western Railway, as the successor to the London & Southampton, continued to build to Tite's basic design for the next thirty years. The 1866/68 main building at St Deny's was one of the best

examples of Tite style construction. They were in red brick, with rusticated quoining, and a projecting roof. If entrusted to untalented hands, this style can become box-like, but at one end there is a shallow projection on to the platform and forecourt elevations, creating a shallow T. Our portrait, taken on 24 July 1972, reveals how well the LSWR engineers' office interpreted the Tite theme at St Deny's. Whilst most of this group of buildings were excellent, the proportions sometimes went awry, as at Andover Junction and Fordingbridge. Nevertheless, they provided a recognisable house style that characterised many LSWR stations throughout the company's existence and long thereafter. The Morris Minor, Ford Anglia and Mini provide a perfect gallery of 1950s and 1960s classic cars.

Opposite bottom: Four tracks extended from the divergence of the Southampton Central and Southampton Town routes as far as St Deny's, where the westernmost pair of tracks continued north to Winchester and London, the eastern pair of tracks curving sharply to the east, to Netley and Fareham. We are looking from platform 3, the Down Netley, towards the divergence and platform 4. In the early days, LSWR canopies were often supported on square wooden pillars, but unlike many railways where such early structures were replaced, some survived into BR days. Later on, wooden posts gave way to typical Victorian fluted cast iron columns, and eventually to rolled steel joists and reinforced concrete.

Above: In the 1860s, the LNWR decided that enlargement of Liverpool (Lime St) station was necessary, whilst a prestigious hotel adjoining the station was another must. In 1867, the first of two magnificent trainsheds was erected at Lime St, to the designs of William Baker, who was born in 1817, and had been engineer-in-charge of new works since Robert Stephenson's death in 1859. Although Baker was chief engineer, his principal assistant, Francis Stevenson, also had a major role in the design. Stevenson was another talented engineer, who took over as chief engineer after Baker died on 20 December 1878, holding the post until his own death in January 1902. The crescent-trussed trainshed, which was carried on cast iron Doric columns, has a clear span of no less than 219 feet, and was joined in 1874 by a matching trainshed with a 186 foot span to provide covered accommodation for nine platforms and three central stabling roads. The two trainsheds are outstanding, and quite rightly have been accorded listed protection. This 1974 view is looking towards the 131 yard long Russell St tunnel that has always constricted the station throat.

Opposite bottom: William Baker succeeded Robert Stephenson as engineer to the LNWR, and the trainshed at Lime Street is a testimonial to his skills. The Station hotel was the work of another celebrated Victorian. Alfred Waterhouse was born at Aigburth on Merseyside on 19 July 1830, and trained as an architect, entering practice in Manchester in 1853. The Manchester Assize Courts in 1859 assured his prestige, and in a career that spanned fifty years, he specialised in Victorian Gothic Revival architecture, but ventured into other styles, French Neo-Renaissance being another style where he excelled. Waterhouse retired in 1902, passing away on 22 August 1905. The LNWR chose this celebrated architect with roots on Merseyside for the North Western Hotel, which was completed in 1871. It is in Renaissance style, with strong vertical lines that impel the eye upwards. At first, the decoration is restrained, so the eye sweeps upwards, but after the prominent cornice that tops the fifth floor, the building explodes into a riot of decoration, with dormer windows, ornate chimney stacks and pyramid turrets, with two spires towering above the central section. Ornamental iron railings, or cresting, crown the corner pyramids, completing a magnificent structure. The interior, with over 200 rooms, was furnished in French Renaissance style to match the exterior. It served as a railway hotel for a century, but then fell on evil times. As a listed building, it was saved from demolition and now provides 246 student flats for Liverpool John Moore's University. The combination of William Baker,

Stevenson and Waterhouse should have produced a winning combination, and I wish I could say it did. My father was born on Merseyside, as were his father and grandfather. His great grandfather, Dr Daniel Hendry, who was born in Paisley in 1824, had moved to Liverpool to set up a medical dynasty that includes his wife and daughter, who were two of the first fifty women to qualify in medicine. My father spent his early years on Merseyside, and knew Exchange and Lime St stations before 1923. Naturally, he had a soft spot for Liverpool, and loved Lime St, but the overall effect did not work. The hotel fronts on to Lime St, but masks the older northern trainshed. The second trainshed is set back from the road in an uninspiring cul-de-sac, which for many years was disfigured by a bungalow growth of station offices, which however useful, looked dreadful. The removal of these shanties has improved the effect, but even so, these magnificent buildings do not sit together happily, and Lime St is a potent example of how buildings must harmonise if they are to be seen to their best advantage.

Below: On many small railways, raising money was a problem. One such company was the Isle of Man Railway, which was formed in 1870 to build lines from Douglas to Peel, Port Erin and Ramsey. When fund raising was slow, the IMR dropped the Ramsey line, and brought in mainland railway financiers, who controlled the company for over thirty years. With no money for masonry buildings or raised platforms,

ground level access to trains had to suffice. Although Douglas and Peel were later replaced, the original 1873 timber buildings survived at the wayside stations until the line closed in 1968. Crosby station, seen on 21 August 1967, is a remarkable time warp. Other than being relocated closer to the level crossing in the 1890s, an easy job with a timber structure, it had scarcely altered since the day the railway opened ninety-four years earlier. Contemporary accounts described the buildings as being in the 'New English' or 'Swiss Chalet' style. All were distinguished by large diamond shaped zinc roofing tiles, gable ends and an overhanging roof. The building was divided into two sections, the near portion with double doors being the general waiting room. This was provided with a brick built chimney and fireplace. The other half was divided into a Ladies Waiting room, a Booking Clerk's office, and a diminutive space for porters. Train control on the single line was by a telegraph instrument which was housed in the booking office, along with the ticket cabinets, dating stamp and a desk for the clerk, a remarkable achievement in an office that measuring 8 feet by 9 feet. An internal toilet was provided for ladies, but gents had the customary open air urinal, to the left of the building. A drumhead clock was provided on the front elevation. The station facilities included a passing loop and a couple of sidings, one of which terminates in the bush to the left of the building. One fears that this would be a somewhat flimsy buffer stop in the event of a wagon over-running.

A NEW REALITY
1875–1900

By the start of the 1870s, the pioneering age of railways was over. George and Robert Stephenson were both gone, as was Brunel, along with the other great names from the dawn of the railway age. Most main lines had been created by 1875, with just a few to follow in the next twenty-five years. As railways settled into the landscape, railway officers could draw on years of experience, a better awareness of what made economic sense, and what was extravagant. Some of the stations of the 1840s and 1850s had been far more opulent than prudence warranted, and by the 1870s, railway officers were more cautious. However the period we are about to look at included some magnificent stations, and commenced with one of the most romantic and spectacular railway lines ever built in the British Isles. It finished in the same way.

Below: At about the time that John Sydney Crossley was born at Loughborough on Christmas Day 1812, Napoleon's troops were reeling back from their disastrous attack on Russia. Momentous events were to feature in Crossley's life, with tragedy never far away. He was an orphan within two years, but by the age of twenty, was engineer to the Leicester Canal Co. Soon he was working for the Leicester & Swannington Railway, one of the precursors of the Midland Railway, and in 1857 he became engineer to the Midland Railway. A few years later, he was to drive a railway across the barren

northern fells. Its name, the Settle & Carlisle Railway, became a legend, and Crossley virtually worked himself to death to build it. It is said that after an inspection trip in an open wagon, he remarked 'Finis Coronat Opus'. That was in 1875. Crossley's masterpiece, the Settle & Carlisle Railway opened on May Day 1876. Within three years, Crossley was dead. By the 1960s, it looked like his line would die too. Dr Beeching had no use for it, and if you read the Beeching report, the musical names of the lovely stations that Crossley built appear, as does the brief entry Carlisle – Skipton. It was to die, but unlike most lines, the Settle & Carlisle refused to die quietly. It just kept on going, until it became too prestigious, and eventually too useful, to shut. Lazonby, one of the medium sized stations provided by Crossley, typifies this group of buildings, and I have selected a portrait taken just after sunrise on an autumn morning as passengers are awaiting the early train to Carlisle to represent them.

Opposite top: Until 1870, GWR stations had varied greatly in quality. Some, including Culham, (see page16) Charlbury or Southam Road & Harbury, all of which were the work of Brunel, were inspired. Others were less impressive, and Oxford, which deserved better, given the architectural quality of the town, and the traffic it saw, had to make do with a long wooden pavilion from 1852 to 1972. Throughout this early period, variety had been the keynote. By the mid-1870s, a standardised approach was apparent. Red brick was used for long life and economy, and ornamentation was kept to a minimum. Shallow hipped roofs were normal, although a number of stations in the London area received steeply pitched roofs and French renaissance towers. Langley, although

located in Buckinghamshire, is 16 miles west of Paddington, so is part of the London commuter belt, and lies between West Drayton and Slough. It is a notable example of the French renaissance chateau style, and was the work of Lancaster Owen, and dates from 1878/79. Only the Up Relief platform retains the 1870s buildings, but they are splendid, although the white paintwork on the brick in this 1989 study is not helpful, nor is the drab green paint on the canopy. If this building is compared to Cholsey on page 47, the first impression is that there is nothing in common, but a closer inspection reveals the exact opposite. The treatment of the roof is different, Cholsey receiving the usual shallow hipped roof, but the chimney stacks are identical, as are the brick courses below the roofline. The fretwork on the canopy is the same, though the way the end deepens at Cholsey is more elegant than at Langley. Owen showed considerable ingenuity in developing a standard building in a highly individual manner.

Opposite bottom: As with so many stations, general freight facilities were withdrawn in 1964, but Total Oil (GB) Ltd established a large fuel depot at the east end of the station, served off the up and down relief lines. With a modern image layout, a general goods yard is unlikely, but a dedicated terminal of this sort is feasible, though it would need to be modelled in low relief. I have included this view as it may help modellers, and the different colours of the tanks give a touch of variety. The four aspect colour light in the foreground, S131, S indicating Slough power signal box, controls movements on the up relief. A two aspect subsidiary signal is bracketed on to the post to control movements into the reception road, which also functions as an Up Refuge Siding.

Opposite top: Before the Railway Age, Market Harborough was an important coaching town, and prior to the Beeching cuts, this importance persisted, as lines radiated from the town in six directions. The first to arrive was the LNWR Rugby & Stamford branch, which was formally opened from Rugby on 27 April 1850, and extended to Rockingham, five miles to the east on 1 June 1850. On 2 June 1851 the line reached Luffenham, where it connected with the MR line to Peterborough. In 1857, the MR main line was extended from Leicester to Bedford and Hitchin, where it joined the Great Northern Railway to reach King's Cross. Midland trains ran over North Western metals for three quarters of a mile at Market Harborough, but the delays caused by these flat junctions became so bad that the companies obtained powers in 1881 to build a flyover carrying the LNWR over the MR, and to erect a new joint station in the V of the divergence of the Rugby and Bedford lines, was opened on 14 September 1884, the flyover following in 1885. In the meanwhile, the LNWR had completed a branch from Northampton to Market Harborough in 1859. In 1879, the LNWR and GN Joint line was completed from Melton Mowbray to a triangular junction at Welham just outside the town. The main building at the 1884 station resembled a Queen Anne mansion, Queen Anne reigning from 1702 to 1714, a period when the flowery styles of the late Jacobean era of the Stuarts were moving towards the classicism of Georgian and Regency architecture. The Queen Anne style was not used to any great extent for railway work, but was well suited to Market Harborough, the

converging embankments leading the eye naturally towards the building. We see the station on 1 October 1972. By this time, the LNW & GN joint line had long gone, as had the Rugby & Stamford branch, but the Northampton & Market Harborough line remained in use for freight and a single northbound passenger train each evening. The Rail Express Parcels van is a reminder of the days when the railways undertook collection and delivery by road to provide a complete transport service.

Opposite bottom: The booking hall, which was at road level, was connected to the central island platform by a covered incline and to the platforms on either side by subways. We are looking towards Leicester from the Northbound Midland platform on 1 October 1972. Platform No 1, on the right, handled southbound Midland services to St Pancras. The inclined ramp in blue engineering bricks visible in the distance carried a roadway across the LNWR and Midland tracks to provide access from the town to the MR goods depot to the right of the running lines. Apart from providing an incline down to the yard, the arches beneath it acted as stables for the Midland cartage horses at Market Harborough. I could never find out if a story I was told that horses were graded according to height, the tallest being placed in the most northerly stables, was true or not. It would be lovely if this were so, but I have my doubts. The LNWR goods yard was on the opposite side of the line out of view. By the time this view was taken, the access road had been closed and the bridge removed. An alternative access to the MR yard existed via a narrow lane that flanked the

station on the right. The Queen Anne Mansion has survived, but modern buildings have long since replaced the platform buildings and the lovely awning.

Below: Two separate goods sheds were provided at Market Harborough, the Midland shed being much the larger, but the LNWR shed was quite commodious, as we see here. The triple louvers in the end gable were common on LNWR goods sheds, and provided ventilation without the complexities and expense of the clerestory ventilator used on some structures. One track ran through the shed, emerging behind the single story block which projects at the right end of the structure. This was used by the goods agent as his office. The building to the right of the signal is on the far side of the main line, and is the old MR goods shed. The mossy area in the foreground is the site of two sidings. Sidings in goods yards were usually arranged in pairs, with a space for road vehicles for loading and unloading purposes, after which there might be another pair of tracks. The Midland yard had two such pairs of tracks, the outermost serving a long cattle pen. The LNWR yard at Market Harborough was an awkward shape, as St Mary's churchyard projected into it, taking a triangular bite from the centre of the yard. Side and end loading facilities and the cattle dock were at the Rugby end of the 'bite', and the goods shed and general sidings at the Stamford end. A modeller who is confronted with an awkward site, for example a chimney, could use this prototype, with rising ground, trees and a low relief building to disguise the chimney.

Below: The River Dee rises high in the Cairngorms, some 4000 feet above sea level, and after falling steeply, becomes a broad and beautiful river, flowing east to reach the sea at Aberdeen. For a little over a century, the last forty miles of the Dee was paralleled by a railway line, and because Queen Victoria's husband, Prince Albert, had an eye for beautiful scenery and had bought an estate at Balmoral in Upper Deeside, a royal connection began, that still endures today. The first 16¾ miles, from Aberdeen to Banchory was opened in September 1853. At first, the line had been intended to stretch as far as Aboyne, some 32 miles west of Aberdeen, but financial difficulties precluded this. Aboyne remained the target of the Deeside Railway, and the Aboyne Extension was authorised in 1857, and opened on 2 December 1859. The Aboyne & Braemar Railway was authorised in 1865 to access the timber of upper Deeside, and because of the growing tourist potential of the North of Scotland. The line was opened as far as Ballater, 43¼ miles from Aberdeen, on 17 October 1866. Some work was carried out west of Ballater, but the purchase by Queen Victoria of Ballochbuie Forest meant that timber traffic was now unlikely, so the extension plans were dropped. The Royal connection, although ensuring that the line would not be extended to Braemar, gave immense prestige to Deeside, and when a local Aboyne resident, Sir Cunliffe Brooks, established a golf club here in 1883, the town started to develop as a fashionable resort. The Great North of Scotland Railway had leased the Deeside Railway for 999 years in 1866, and embarked on a spectacular rebuild of the station in 1888. The new station was in Scottish baronial style, with round granite towers at each end of the main building, topped with conical spires. The Mk IX Jaguar, which

belonged to my mother, seems at home in this impressive environment.

Opposite top: The Deeside Railway received its death sentence in the Beeching Report, and passenger services were withdrawn on 28 February 1966, freight services lingering on until July. We are looking east towards Aberdeen shortly after the end of traffic, whilst the line was awaiting its fate. Had it survived a few years longer, it is probable it would still be in existence, as economic activity around Aberdeen and suburban growth means a heavy commuter traffic to and from the granite city. The main buildings on the left survive at Aboyne, having been converted into a range of shops. Thankfully they retain much of their character, but sadly the platforms, the canopies, footbridge, and other infrastructure have all been swept away. A short section of the Deeside Railway is being rebuilt as a heritage line, but sadly I doubt if trains will ever traverse the full 43 miles of the Deeside railway which has some stunning views of the river that are not obtainable from the nearby road, superb though that is.

Opposite bottom left: Cholsey & Moulsford station, which is located between Reading and Didcot on the GWR main line, and was the junction of the Wallingford branch for many years, typifies Great Western stations built in the last quarter of the nineteenth century, and which did much to develop a GWR house style. The buildings, which date from 1892, were the work of J W Armstrong, and replaced an earlier station located about three quarters of a mile closer to Paddington. They are in the mellow red brick favoured by the GWR for many years, and feature a canopy cantilevered out from the walls, avoiding the inconvenience of support

pillars on the platform, which impede passenger flow, and the movement of luggage trolleys. The windows have concrete lintels, with relieving arches above each group of windows in engineers' blue brick. This grouping also applies where a window and door adjoin one another, so that although there are nine window or door openings, there are but five relieving arches. The building at Langley, previously illustrated, although superficially quite different, repeats many of these design features, and includes similar relieving arches although the white masonry paint at Langley makes them harder to see. Scorned by many architects in later years, these buildings were neat, functional and economical to maintain. These were the qualities that commended them to the Chief Civil Engineer, and the survival of many of these unadventurous but sound buildings for well over 100 years suggests that the GWR got it right. We are looking at the building on platform 4 on 27 July 1989.

Opposite bottom right: At first sight, the station appears to be a typical single story GWR building, but the line is on an embankment, and the station frontage is a two-story structure, the staircase having particularly fine leaf pattern cast iron balusters to support the hand rail. The steps, which had originally been stone, had suffered wear from countless thousands of feet over the years, and had been built up in cement, with a steel edging, as unprotected cement will soon crumble under such an onslaught. At the time of our visit in July 1989, the station was undergoing long overdue repairs, as the state of the cement indicates only too clearly. Although this is a view that one tends to pass by, there is much of interest. The end baluster before the wall is angled, as the

banister rail is turned inwards. The steel capping plate cannot extend to the end of the stair because of the balusters, so stops short, leaving the edge of the step without protection from crumbling. The second handrail that descends in the other direction shows that the staircase reverses at a landing behind us. Conscious that a tall flight of stairs poses a risk

in the event of a fall, the Board of Trade insisted on landings if the height of stairs exceeded 10 feet. Further rules specified that no step was to have a tread of less than 11 inches, or a rise of less than seven inches. These figures, though seemingly of little interest to the modeller, can be used to estimate the dimensions of buildings that vanished long ago. If there is one

intermediate landing, it will usually be at the mid point. If there are two landings, they will usually divide the staircase into three equal sections. If a photo enables you to see the number of steps to the first landing, an informed guess as to the height of the stairs is possible.

Above: The railway age saw an explosion of economic activity and of population growth, and within a decade of completing its London extension to St Pancras in 1868, the Midland Railway found it was playing a game of catch up, enlarging its stations and providing additional running lines. Leicester, which had enjoyed phenomenal growth from the 1840s, was a particular bottleneck, and the station was rebuilt at the start of the 1890s. Charles Trubshaw, who had trained as an architect under his father, also called Charles, who was architect and surveyor to Stafford County Council, became an Associate of the Royal Institute of British Architects in 1865, and worked for the LNWR until 1874, when he joined the Midland Railway. His early work included Hellifield and Skipton stations, but Leicester (London Road) as the new station was named, was his finest work. The frontage, which was completed in 1892, is in red brick, set off with ornately moulded orange-brown terracotta. The road is climbing at this point, and numerous arches, which provide pedestrian and vehicular access to two separate covered carriage bays, pierce the frontage. One porte cochere, as such shelters are known, was for arrivals, the other for departures. A balustrade, with regularly spaced urns, tops the frontage. The frontage terminates in a hexagonal clock tower, pierced with opening windows and supporting small balconies. Without this feature, the structure would be

fussy, but lack any strong visual climax. The design is highly ornate, and with equally magnificent structures at Derby and Nottingham, and the incomparable splendour of St Pancras, the Midland passenger arrived and departed from some of the most ornate and flamboyant temples to the railway age ever created. We are looking away from the city centre on 13 September 1972.

Opposite top: Behind the façade, the two bay ridge and furrow roof was carried across the carriage drive without any intermediate supports to provide a clear vehicular access. In later years, one piece rolled steel joists might have been used, but at this date, riveted girders were still preferred. The entrances, which are seen on 22 July 1971, could be closed by ornamental iron gates, a number of engineering firms specialising in supplying intricate patterns. The balustrade in the right foreground adds to an already eye catching structure. Charles Trubshaw retired in 1905, and died at Derby, where he had lived and worked for so long on 15 February 1917. His frontage is deservedly a Grade 2 listed structure.

Opposite centre: Our next view, from London Road Junction signal box, gives an idea of the confined site into which the station had to be shoehorned. It was taken during a blizzard on 28 November 1973. Snow may look pretty on a Christmas card, but to railwaymen, it ranks with

the biblical pestilences visited upon the pharaohs of ancient Egypt. The murky visibility gives an idea as to why this is so. London Road Junction controlled the southern end of the station, and the bridge that is visible through the murk is London Road, with Trubshaw's screen rising above it. The location of the box was determined by the constraints of the site, but was inconvenient. Access to the box, through the bridge openings was dangerous and awkward, and the signalman had no view of the platforms because of the road bridge. Partly because of the access problems, visits to London Road box were seldom permitted, but there was another reason. The inspector accompanying my father and myself warned us that if we heard gunfire, we should dive for cover. Seeing our look of disbelief, he explained that local yobs in a nearby high rise building sometimes took shots at the signal box and railwaymen going to or from it. We edged along the access wall, and then made a concerted rush for the box. The signalman, though openly incredulous that anyone would voluntarily want to visit his battle zone in the middle of a blizzard, made us welcome. The box, which was gable roofed, was an LMS designed box developed from the earlier Midland style, but with a brick base. It housed a 50 lever frame, virtually all of which was still working at the time of our visit. The box was one of two controlling the station, the other being Leicester North.

Below right: Many enthusiasts find it difficult to understand the signalling at a large station, so I have portrayed the illumined track circuit diagram to show how it was done. The upper tracks are the passenger lines, the two lower tracks being the up and down goods lines, which skirt the passenger station. In case you are wondering what happened to 'the junction', the Midland regarded a connection between fast and slow lines as 'a junction' as lines joined one another, hence the name of the south box. The signals are a mixture of colour light and semaphore. Up signal No 11 has a 'feather' controlling movements over crossover No 3 to the Down Goods. No 12/14 signal is provided with a route indicator to display platform data. At most stations, the signal controlling entry to the platform would be the home signal or inner home, and there would be a departure signal or starter at the far end of the platform, controlling entry to the next section and the next box, but at large stations worked by more than one box, the platform is often 'the section', so 12/14 are the starters to Leicester North box via platforms 1 and 2. In semaphore days, there would have been two separate arms, worked by levers 12 or 14. The rectangular box with two diagonal circles is a subsidiary calling on signal, to indicate to the driver that he must enter the platform with caution, expecting to find it already occupied. In semaphore days this would have been a pair of small subsidiary arms, but here we have lights and the route indicator. In absolute block working, not more than one train can be in the section between boxes at any time, but at a busy station, where trains may combine or split, this is impracticable, and a different system applies. On freight only lines under Permissive Block regulations, more than one train can be in the section, the signalman accepting the first train, and when he received the entering section bell, putting his block instrument to Train on Line. If a further train is offered to him, he can accept it under a special Permissive acceptance code, and will turn the special commutator or knob on his block instrument to Position 2. If a third train is offered he advances it to position 3, and so on. When a train clears the section, he blocks out in the usual way and reduces the score by one train, until he gets back to the Line Blocked position. In busy passengers stations controlled by multiple signal boxes, permissive working was adopted, but was called Station Yard Working if applied to passenger lines. The block instruments below the diagram are BR 'bakelite' instruments, with a nine position Permissive counter, and are unidirectional instruments, accepting trains on the Up platform lines 3 and 4, which is why they only have one needle section, as they are only used for acceptance. The splitting semaphore signals, 34/40 and 38/39 control movements in the UP direction out of platforms 4, 3, 2 and 1 respectively. The previous illustration reveals that they are genuine MR timber post signals that will be at least 50 years old.

Below: The frames in most standard LMS boxes were based on Midland practice with a raised quadrant plate and a locking section above floor level behind the frame, this permitting a lower structure than other designs. No 1 lever is red, so works a signal, and controls the 'feather' on No 11, the home signal, to route movements over crossover No 3 from the down main to the down goods. No 3 lever, which works these points, is painted black. BoT regulations required all facing points on passenger lines to be locked, so that they could not move under a train. Lever No 2, which is blue, works the Facing Point Lock, or FPL. No 4 is a red lever, and reference to the diagram will show that it is located under the left hand road bridge next to the Up passenger line. It controls wrong direction setting back moves over crossover No 5 to the goods lines, or to dwarf or shunt signal No 9. Signals 12 and 14 are red with a white band, which indicates that they are released by the block instruments, and are the starting signals through platforms 1 and 2 to Leicester North box. The white levers in the distance, No's 31 and 43, are spares, whilst the yellow levers, 36 and 42 are the UP distant signals at the far end of the station. They are semaphore signals, and can only be pulled if the signalman has accepted a train from Leicester North, and has offered it on to the next box and had it accepted, and has set the road and pulled all his running signals. Until he has done so, the locking will prevent him clearing the distant signal. A driver seeing the distant off, can run with confidence, knowing that he has a clear road through the station and to the next box, though this does not absolve him from the duty of looking for each signal just in case an emergency has arisen, and the signalman has to stop him. Should he encounter an adverse signal after he has seen the distant, he knows he must make an emergency stop.

Bottom: Just as London Road defined the southern limits of Leicester passenger station, Swain St bridge marked the northern end of the platforms, the passenger lines coming together beyond the bridge. We are looking from Leicester North box towards the station on 30 July 1971. On the far left is the Up Sidings shunt spur, the two lines disappearing on the left providing access to the loco sidings. The second line running beneath the bridge is the Up Goods, the Down Goods passing between the bridge pier and the Mk 2 carriage, which is at the end of the shunting siding. This siding, which is reached from the far end of the station, is controlled by London Road Junction. The double slip in the foreground is worked by levers 43 and 47, and provides a good view of a track formation that was once common at large stations, but which is being replaced by a series of crossovers forming a ladder. The next point on the up main, No 16, controls the divergence into platforms 4 and 3. Further to the right we see the down Island platforms 2 and 1, with

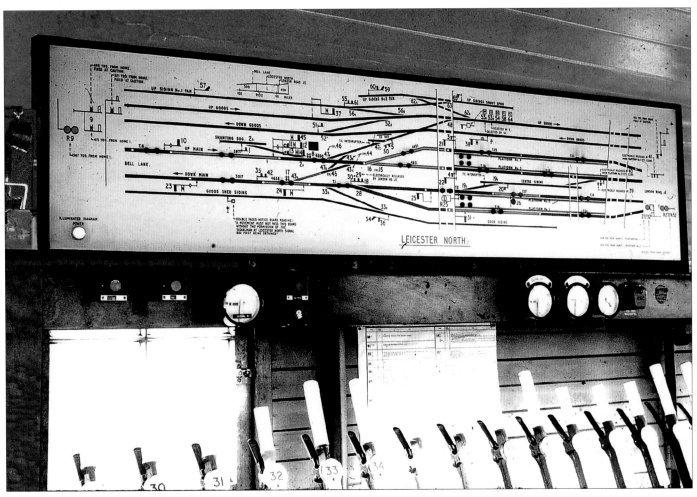

trailing point No 28. Comparing these two crossovers, the mechanism for No 16 looks more complex. This is a facing point on a passenger line, and is provided with a facing point lock, lever No 15. At this time, there was no facing cross-over permitting southbound trains to enter platforms 2 or 1. As wrong direction movements were NOT possible into these platforms, a facing point lock was not needed. If single line working was instituted because of a derailment or during engineering work, the points were clamped, so they could not move or be pulled whilst a train was passing over them. To the right of platform 1 is Campbell St goods depot, which was the site of the original Leicester station. The triple shunt discs, Nos 18, 29 and 30, control wrong direction shunt movements into the down platform lines, and have white diamonds on the red band because they are 'Rule 55 exempt'. Rule 55 was introduced after several accidents when a signalman brought a train to a stand at a signal and then forgot about it, and accepted another train which ran into the back of it. As a result, Rule 55 provided that the driver had to send the fireman to the box to remind the signalman of his presence. When track circuits were introduced, the BoT agreed that they made this precaution unnecessary, signals that were exempt from Rule 55 being indicated by a white diamond. Enthusiasts are sometimes puzzled by how to read a row of vertical shunt signals, but there is a simple rule. The letters BR LT give the answer. BR - Bottom Right; LT Left

Top. In a vertical row of signals, the bottom signal refers to the right hand road, and the top signal to the left hand road. The bottom signal in this triplet, No 30 controls setting back moves into the right hand platform No 1, and the middle signal controls moves into platform No 2. As the platform lines constitute the section between boxes, both are electrically released by London Road Junction.

Above: Visits to the Leicester boxes were seldom permitted, and it was many years before we did so, visiting Leicester North on 30 July 1971. Compared with London Road junction, the diagram is mirror imaged, but this depends on which way the frame faces in the box, and as the signalman is only in one box at any time, is not a problem in day-to-day working, though it makes it harder to compare adjacent boxes. In the previous caption, I referred to the triple shunt signals 18, 29 and 30. They appear as three miniature semaphore arms in this view. The top arm, No 18 controls movements over No 19 crossover into the centre siding. As this is not a running line, it is not electrically released by London Road junction, although London Road does control the exit points at the far end of the siding. This means that there are six running lines between the boxes, the up and down goods, the two up platforms and the two down platforms, and one through siding. On the left side of the diagram, the Up Main home signal, No 10, is shown with a diamond on the post. This is a Rule 55 exempt diamond

post. This is a Rule 55 exempt diamond indicating that the line is track circuited by red coloured track circuit T6. Semaphore signals are customarily shown in the danger horizontal position, but at the top of the diagram, signal No 57 is shown in the off position. This indicates that 'it normally stands off' or is in the pulled position, permitting trains to move past it. It permits movements out of the Up Sidings No 1 Fan, the points there being controlled by hand levers, so do not appear on the diagram. A train must not pass a signal at danger, and if this signal were in the normal position, every time a move took place out of the sidings, the signalman would have to pull it, diverting attention from signalling train movements. However, a move must not take place from the sidings when a move is taking place into the loco yards, so the signalman will put 57 to danger before a move is signalled to or from the loco yard. The Goods Shed Siding, which adjoins the Down Main, shows another unusual feature. A double-sided notice board reads, 'A movement must not pass this board without the permission of the signalman at Leicester North Signal Box first being obtained.' No 34 signal, which is from the Dock Siding, also stands off, as it controls movements from the Dock Siding and up to the notice board. No 36 signal, which is on the same post, stands normal, and when a move is signalled to the running lines, No 34 is put to danger, points No 33 are pulled, and then No 36 signal is pulled to permit the move. The red lights in Platform No 2 indicate that a train is occupying the platform.

Above: John Thomas wrote of the railways of his native Scotland with an enchanting mix of passion and attention to detail. I read his account of the January day in 1889 when seven men gathered at Spean Bridge to cross Rannoch Moor, but as I did so, and realised how the party was nearly lost through a combination of lashing rain, mist and gales, one might have been with them. More than a century later, Elena and I walked from Rannoch station to the viaduct that lies to the north. It was a warm sunny day, yet within minutes, we were squelching through the boggy ground that makes up the Moor, and I thought of the events of long ago. One of that party was a resourceful young Scottish engineer called Charles de Neuville Forman (1852-1901), and it was his engineering skill that drove the North British backed West Highland Railway across the hundred miles between Craigendoran and Fort William, crossing the moor that had so nearly claimed his life. Charles Forman had been born in Glasgow in 1852, and after education at Glasgow University trained with the family business, being admitted as a partner in 1875. He was resilient and quick witted, a good engineer on the ground, and a polished performer in parliamentary debates, especially where there was opposition. Restless and determined, Charles Forman was a workaholic, and his excessive workload led to his health collapsing, and a trip to recuperate at Davos Platz in Switzerland was unsuccessful, Forman dying there on 8 February 1901, at the early age of 48. The West Highland opened in 1894, and its stations read like a roll call of Scottish history, Garelochead, Arrochar & Tarbet,

Crianlarich, Rannoch, Tulloch and Fort William. Rannoch had not existed as a place before the coming of the railway, and a 40 mile road had to be built across the moor to service the construction depot located here. After the navvies departed, its sole purpose was as a block post and to provide a base for PW men. The West Highland Railway employed James Miller, (1860-1947), a young architect who had worked for the Caledonian for a time before setting up in practice in 1892. Miller received the commission for the main buildings for the WHR, and on the island platforms that Charles Forman provided, Miller designed a single story building with a brick base and timber superstructure topped with a concave roof that overhangs the building to provide a canopy. It was built in the Swiss chalet style, which enjoyed popularity in late Victorian days.

Opposite top: The Belfast & Ballymena Railway opened in April 1848. It was a curious railway, as it connected the two places in its title by means of a reversal at Carrickfergus Junction, some six miles north of Belfast. In due course, the main line reached Londonderry, 95 miles from Belfast, whilst the Carrickfergus line was continued on to Larne, where a ferry port was to develop, and the line became the Belfast & Northern Counties Railway. Five years after the B&B opened, a baby was born in the South of Ireland in Co Wexford. His name was Berkeley Deane Wise, and in due course he joined the local Dublin, Wicklow & Wexford Railway. In 1877, he was appointed resident engineer to the Belfast & Co Down Railway, and in 1888, he became civil engineer to the Belfast & Northern

Counties Railway. He was a meticulous civil engineer, an innovative signal engineer and a talented architect with a flair for creating distinctive buildings. After rebuilding Larne and Portrush stations, he turned his attention to Carrickfergus when the station had burned down in 1895. The new building was in the fashionable 'Domestic Revival' style, in which a mock half-timbered structure on a brick base recalled an idealised world of Tudor cottages and domestic simplicity. It was a reaction to the excesses of High Victorian Gothic, Jacobean and Tudor, in which ever-more decorative interpretations of past glories were created. The domestic revivalists sought to recapture a purer and simpler age. Tall ornately panelled chimneys, tiled, rather than slated roofs, and a tile-hung section above the upper window in the main gable provided a striking building. We see Carrickfergus station on 28 August 1967.

Opposite bottom: Berkeley Wise had forceful ideas about signalling. When on the Co Down, he patented a divisible train staff that saved the costs of electric train staff equipment, whilst avoiding the risks inherent in single line train staff and ticket working, if station staff and enginemen were careless of the rules. Wise believed that the somersault signal was safer than other types, and his somersault signals were to dominate the BNCR and its successors for as long as semaphore signals existed on the system. Finally Wise believed that it was important to provide the best possible visibility for signalmen. Generous windows and a pronounced overhang to the roof shaded the windows from direct sunlight for most of the

day, with the added advantage of keeping the box cool in summer. In recent years, many signal boxes have had replacement double glazing units fitted, and a complaint I have heard from signalmen is that as only a few windows can now be opened, their boxes act as greenhouses. Berkeley Wise solved that

problem long ago. We see Carrickfergus box on 25 August 1966. The platform canopies repeat the domestic revival theme of the main buildings. The Belfast & Northern Counties Railway was purchased by the Midland Railway in 1903, becoming the Midland Railway Northern Counties Committee. In 1923, it

became the LMS NCC, and on 1 January 1948, it was inherited by the Railway Executive, as the RE NCC, but it had already been agreed that the line would be transferred to the statutory road and rail authority in Northern Ireland, the Ulster Transport Authority, later Northern Ireland Railways.

Opposite top: If you study an old railway map, a group of lines belonging to the Manchester, Sheffield & Lincolnshire Railway, later the Great Central Railway, run from Wrexham to Connah's Quay, and through the centre of the Wirral peninsula. They are separated from the rest of the GC by some 40 miles, and are only accessible by running powers over the Cheshire Lines Committee in which the GC had an interest. The section from Connah's Quay to Bidston, on the outskirts of Birkenhead, was authorised at various times from 1884, but in 1895, the Dee & Birkenhead Railway was renamed the North Wales & Liverpool Railway, and construction began. Sir Douglas and Francis Fox were appointed engineers with Monk & Newell as contractors, and the line was opened to freight on 16 March 1896, with a formal opening attended by the celebrated Liberal leader, W E Gladstone, on 28 March 1896. Public services began on 18 May 1896, the line being worked by MS&L engines which had been given Wrexham, Mold & Connah's Quay lettering for legal reasons! In 1904, the Great Central Railway secured powers to absorb the WM&CQ, the Buckley Railway and NW&L with effect from 1 January 1905. Neston station opened in 1896 with the rest of the line, and was later renamed Neston & Parkgate and then Neston North. The line was proposed for closure under the Beeching plan, and Neston lost its freight services but passenger services survived. Wooden platforms and narrow brick buildings devoid of any ornament, save for a pair of matching louvered ventilators that tower over what had been the toilet blocks, were provided, as we see in this portrait looking towards Bidston in 1988.

Opposite bottom: From the station approach, the building offered a strange appearance, with a door at pavement level, and windows scattered seemingly at random at four different levels. The lower portion of the building was supported on arches that also differed. A chimney was built at an angle to the building, as the two sections were not in line, and there was also a different roof level between the two sections. An old joke claims that on account of its ungainly appearance, a camel is a horse designed by a committee, and Neston has similar qualities. Had I encountered a structure like this on a model railway, I would have doubted its authenticity, but however bizarre it is, here is the proof. Apart from the peculiar road elevation, this scene, when considered with the previous illustration, is useful to the modeller as it shows the construction of a traditional timber platform on a low embankment.

Below: The Lancashire, Derbyshire & East Coast Railway came in with a bang and went out with a whimper. The company was incorporated in August 1891 with powers to build a 170 mile main line from the Manchester Ship Canal at Warrington to a new port at Sutton on the east coast, and would have included a 300 foot high viaduct in Monsal Dale. Only the central section of this astonishing railway, running east from Chesterfield for some 40 miles, was ever built. The proposal received the backing of the GER, as it offered a route from the coalfields to GE territory, and a GE officer, Harry Willmott, was appointed its first general manager in 1895, the first section of the new line opening in 1896. The main line of the LD&ECR eventually ran

from Chesterfield to Pyewipe Junction near Lincoln, and this, with a few short branches bringing the LD&ECR up to 60 route miles, was all that was built of this ambitious scheme. Warsop lies on the edge of the Dukeries district, so named from the number of ducal seats in the area. Warsop station came into use in 1897 when the line into Chesterfield was completed. Most of the intermediate stations on the LD&ECR were substantially built in a hard red brick with a blue engineering brick base, and broad elliptical arches, as at Warsop. Canopies, which were carried on rolled steel joists, provided shelter for passengers, but after closure to passengers, the canopy was cut away. Signalling of the LD&EDR was shared between Saxby & Farmer and the Railway Signal Co, Saxby signalling the main line west of Tuxford, including Warsop station, the box being provided with an ornate fretted bargeboard. The station lay a short distance to the east of Warsop Main Colliery, but there was little industry or population between Warsop and Lincoln, and passenger traffic was disappointing, passenger services ceasing on 19 September 1955, and local freight services ten years later. The LD&ECR was absorbed into the Great Central Railway on 1 January 1907, Harry Willmott, the general manager, going to the East & West Junction Railway, which he reorganised as the Stratford-upon-Avon & Midland Junction Railway. Given the financial troubles of the LD&ECR, it is a little surprising that a more economical approach was not adopted.

Top right: I have called the period from 1875 to 1900 'A New Reality', as railway officers came to grips with the costs of ornate buildings, and country stations increasingly received buildings comparable to Morcott. However, this was not the full story. As the nineteenth century was drawing towards its close, the United Kingdom and its railways were approaching the pinnacle of their prestige and power. At sea, the vast battle fleets of the Royal Navy were the ultimate arbiters of destiny, unchallenged and unchallengeable; on land, the railways enjoyed a comfortable monopoly of inland transport. Neither was expected to change, and although prudent railway officers might be economical at a station such as Morcott, (see page 58), where traffic was never likely to be heavy, no such qualms existed where traffic was already buoyant and likely to rise. Narrow gauge railways are frequently seen as weak, but after its hesitant start when wooden stations such as Crosby had to suffice, the Isle of Man Railway Company had never looked back. Traffic had risen from half a million passengers in 1877 to almost 700,000 passengers within twenty years. The timber chalet at Douglas had gone, replaced by a spectacular new terminal, and at Port St Mary where a timber and corrugated iron shed had sufficed for the first twenty-five years, the Isle of Man Railway decided on a spectacular new brick building that would incorporate living accommodation for the stationmaster on the first floor. Writers have categorised it as a free interpretation of Domestic-Revival-cum-Tudor, but to understand

this remarkable building, we need to know a little of character of the leading players in the story. In this view, which is taken from the access road to the goods yard, we see two segmental arch windows on the ground floor, beyond which is a round-headed window with a pale yellow brick arch. On the first floor, the window surrounds are in yellow brick, separated by stone string courses, the end being topped with a Tudor gable.

Bottom right: The IMR manager, G H Wood, and engineer, Henry Greenbank, had a good working relationship with a leading Manx builder, James Cowle, of St George's St, Douglas. Cowle was painstaking and careful, with a good reputation, one of his trainees, George Preston, (1848–1910), who became a master builder in his own right, being my great grandfather. As with other leading nineteenth century builders on the Island, Cowle also worked as an architect. Although Wood and Greenbank were both strong willed characters, and Greenbank could be extremely prickly, if subjected to criticism from people he did not respect, both men would give remarkable latitude to someone they could rely on. Cowle came in that category. He had been responsible for the design of Douglas station at the start of the 1890s, which had been a spectacular success, and was the obvious choice as architect for Port St Mary. The builder was James Costain, and work started late in 1897, with five interim payments of £200 by July 1898. By then the project was running late. James Cowle, an

obliging and good-natured man, did his best for his fellow builder, with his work certificates. Although the IMR, who had been asked to pay direct for several consignment of bricks to ease Costain's cash flow problems, had done so, they baulked at the next payment, withholding £25 from the balance of £250 due to unfinished work. The final payment, marking the long overdue completion of the building, was in December 1898, making a grand total of £1597 2s 4d. The main frontage presented the remarkable blend of a domestic revival half-timbered gable with a leaded light, below which were a pair of projecting Oriel bay windows topped with a loose trefoil pattern, and separated by a blind arch. Further along, the windows were framed in yellow brick with stone string courses, and there was the Tudor gable we have already seen in the previous view, but above the entrance, the central gable is a mixture of Jacobean and Dutch styles, topped with a curved pediment. Add a shallow tower on the road elevation, a further Oriel bay window that is totally different to its neighbour, and one begins to appreciate the diversity of this fascinating structure.

Below: The purist may say that the fusion of so many styles creates no style, but the building possesses an undeniable charm, and if no architect tried anything different, no new style could ever evolve. This could have been a plain red brick box, but Cowle invested it with a character that suited the Island and the men who ran its railway at the close of the nineteenth century. Therein may lie part of the answer. English and Scottish architecture evolved on quite different lines, as a few minutes in any city north or south of the border will reveal. Not until recent times and the triumph of an International modernism that is devoid of any clear national traits, did English and Scottish architecture merge. The Isle of Man was variously under Viking, Scottish, English and native rule, and its people were a mix of Celt and Viking. Because of the Island's past, Manx architecture absorbed elements from both English and Scottish schools, and with most Manx architects and builders born and trained within that heady mix of styles, it was natural to take freely from both cultures. Once that freedom is admitted, drawing from different schools of thought within one culture is natural. Cowle would be subject to these cross currents, and if we appreciate this, his building then becomes intelligible.

Above: Morcott station was the result of a process that had been gaining momentum on the LNWR for over thirty years. We have seen one of the 1860s timber buildings. Compared with conventional brick structures, they saved time and expense, but there were places where they were too costly for the potential traffic. The LNWR also realised that old coach bodies, although a short-term way to provide mess huts, lamp rooms, and stores, were expensive to maintain as there was no standardisation, given their diverse origins. In 1880, the company introduced a standard prefabricated gable roofed hut. They were 8 feet wide, and could be 8, 16 or 24 foot long, although non-standard lengths were possible. They were vertically planked, and provided with shallow windows two panes deep. The LNWR realised that they could augment existing accommodation at stations or serve as the main station building where the potential traffic was minimal. Some early examples were constructed to the hut format, but by the 1890s, an upmarket version had evolved with horizontal boarding. When the double track LNWR line from Rugby to Luffenham Junction opened in 1851, giving the LNWR access to Stamford, and providing a useful LNWR route from the West Midlands to Peterborough and East Anglia, Morcott was too insignificant to warrant a station. The construction of a direct cut-off from Seaton Junction to the LNWR Northampton & Peterborough line in 1879, placed the 3¾ mile section from Seaton to Luffenham on a sleepy byway, but contrary to what has been said, the line was not singled in 1879, but remained double track. In September 1898, plans were drawn up for a double track station with timber platforms, a couple of sidings worked from a ground frame, and a footbridge to connect the two platforms. On 20 October 1898, the LNWR notified the BoT of their intention to open the

station in eleven days time, asking for the usual inspection. Col H A Yorke, of the Railway Inspectorate visited the station, and in his report, which was written in February 1899, his only requirements were for a clock visible from the platform, and some trailing runaway catchpoints on the up line, due to the gradient. This view of the station approach at Morcott was taken on 4 June 1966, the last day of passenger services on the Rugby–Luffenham Junction line. Stoves provide heating, their cast iron chimneys avoiding the expense of brick fireplaces.

Opposite bottom: The survival of double track on the Seaton Junction – Luffenham Junction section after the construction of the new cut off in 1879 was surprising, as the route carried little traffic, and in 1907, the LNWR decided that the costs of double track could no longer be justified. The line was finally singled, the up line and platform at Morcott being removed. The Down line buildings survived, catering for local traffic until passenger services were withdrawn in June 1966. Freight services had ceased on 4 May 1964, the yard being subsequently lifted. The brick building at the far end of the platform was latterly a store hut, but may have been the base of the signal box that was installed shortly after the station was built in 1898, but which was closed when the line was singled in 1907. Compared with the costly buildings at stations such as Wansford in the 1840s, this more realistic policy enabled the LNWR to serve small communities where a station could not otherwise be justified. The juxtaposition of the nearly contemporaneous Warsop and Morcott stations in this section provides an invaluable commentary on different design trends. The LD&ECR, although hard up

for cash, produced a lavish station although traffic was hardly likely to be heavy, yet within a few years had sold out to the GCR. The LNWR, which was consistently the most profitable of the major pre-grouping companies, was much less lavish in such circumstances, suggesting that North Western management had a clear appreciation of the potential of locations such as Morcott by the closing years of the Victorian era.

Below: The last great main line of the nineteenth century was the London Extension of the Manchester, Sheffield & Lincolnshire Railway. It was part of Sir Edward Watkin's vision of a line from Manchester to London, the Channel coast, and the continent. In pursuit of his dream, Watkin gathered a portfolio of strategic links in the chain he was forging. Foremost was the Manchester, Sheffield & Lincolnshire Railway of which he became chairman. Today the Metropolitan Railway is part of the London Underground, but in its heyday as an independent line, it possessed a main line stretching beyond Aylesbury to terminate at a junction with the LNWR at Verney Junction in rural Buckinghamshire. Watkin was chairman of the Metropolitan. He was chairman of the South Eastern Railway with its routes to Dover and Folkestone. Through the MS&L interest in the Cheshire Lines Committee, he was a member of the CLC, so had access to Merseyside. Add to that the Blackpool Railway, the East London Railway, the Manchester, South Junction & Altrincham, the Neath & Brecon, the Oldham. Ashton-under-Lyne & Guide Bridge, the Sheffield & Midland Joint, and the Wigan Junction Railway, and the scope of Watkin's railway empire is apparent. If you include the Submarine Continental Railway Company, later

the Channel Tunnel Company, an abortive 1880s scheme to create a tunnel that had to wait more than a century for fulfilment, chairmanship of the Voting Trustees of the New York, Lake Erie & Western Railroad, with a 986 mile route from New York to Chicago, and presidency of the Grand Trunk Railway of Canada, an international dimension enters the picture. The idea of a main line that would start north of Nottingham and finish in London was adventurous, but set against Watkin's vision of a rail empire from the American middle-west to the continent, it was almost insignificant. In 1893, the MS&L London Extension was authorised to run from Annesley, just north of Nottingham to Quainton Road, where a junction would be made with Watkin's Metropolitan Railway, branching off when in London, to its own terminus. By now, in his seventies, Watkin's health was failing and in 1894, he reluctantly resigned as chairman of his various railway interests. The MS&L, soon to be re-titled the Great Central Railway, on account of its enlarged scope, set to work to build the line, which was opened with special trains and a grand banquet beneath the trainshed at Marylebone station, the new GC terminus in London, on 9 March 1899. With seventy years experience of building trunk lines, the London Extension was laid out magnificently. Double track from the outset, it was built with quadrupling in mind. Intermediate stations were provided with an Island platform, and highly standardised buildings, reached either from an overbridge or an underbridge. When quadrupling was necessary, the additional tracks would be provided outside the existing lines, bridges having been built with this in mind. We are looking at Brackley Central station on 19 February 1966.

Above: Watkin's dream was condemned at the time and ever since. Was he an irresponsible fool, or did he fail to predict changes in circumstances that were dramatic beyond all belief? The London & Birmingham Railway opened in 1838. The next main line to the north was the Great Northern in 1850. In 1868, the Midland reached London. In the 1870s and 1880s, the LNWR, the Midland and the GNR all started quadrupling large parts of their main lines. If you allow for different routes, such as the LNWR old main line via Kilsby, and the 1880s line through Northampton, or the Midland, with its routes via Leicester and Oakham, and the ramifications of the GNR, traffic growth between London and the north required an additional pair of tracks every ten years from the 1830s to the 1890s. By the start of the 1890s, it would have been prohibitively expensive to widen the existing lines any more. If the rate of growth continued, another four track main line would have been required by 1910. The cheapest way to do that was to build a new route through green fields, and that is what Watkin did. He overlooked two factors. In 1890, freight trains were hauled by small 0-6-0 goods engines, and might be no more than 40-50 wagons in length. By 1900, heavy eight coupled goods engines were multiplying and trains of 80-100 wagons were appearing. An 80 wagon freight takes little more line capacity than a 40 wagon train, so line capacity was almost doubled, staving off the need for a new route, but this was not apparent until after the line was well advanced. In 1890, Watkin failed to appreciate that the motor vehicle would become a potential rival to railways within twenty years. The end for the GC as a through route came in September 1966. Stanier Black Five No 45289 draws water at Rugby Central with the 6.27pm to Marylebone on 16 August 1966. Refuge lines for freight trains have been laid on each side of the running lines, demonstrating how easy it would have been to convert the GC to quadruple track.

Left: The demise of the GC as a through route presaged an orgy of destruction, and whilst the buildings might not have been needed for rail use any more, heartbreaking scenes such as this, taken at Rugby Central in June 1970 showed a profligate waste of fine buildings that could have been put to some use. It was wasteful and irresponsible, and should be a warning to us that vigilence is necessary lest our heritage be destroyed for no reason. We are a little more sensible today, but as will be seen later in this book, there is no room for complacency.

HIGH NOON 1900–1922

In 1900s, railways enjoyed an easy supremacy, their only rivals being electric trams in the big cities, the canals, which were dying, horse drawn vehicles, and the new fangled and unreliable motor vehicle. The big companies were profitable, and although the progress of tramcars and motor vehicles was worrying by 1913, that feeling of supremacy was still there. Traffic was still rising, and railwaymen built for the future. There were a few new lines, but in general it was upgrading existing lines to cope with current and expected demands that attracted the most attention, and in the case of the Great Western, completion of an impressive programme of cut-offs.

Above: Bexhill is mentioned in the Domesday book, but might have remained a small village with its original London Brighton & South Coast Railway station of 1846, had it not been for the 7th Earl de la Warr who transformed it into an exclusive seaside resort, opening the prestigious Sackville Hotel in 1890, Sackville being the family name of the Earl. A new station followed in 1891, but as the town's population more than doubled over the next decade, a third station was opened in Bexhill in 1902. This was a momentous year for the town, which was incorporated as a Borough under the first Royal Charter granted by King Edward VII. To mark this, the 8th Earl de la Warr organised the first motor car races in England along De la Warr Parade, which was then privately owned by the Earl, who got involved in a particularly messy divorce as well in 1902! His son, the 9th Earl, is recalled as the first Socialist mayor in the history of the town, and for commissioning Erich Mendelsohn (1887–1953) and Serge Chermayeff (1900–1996) to create the art deco De la Warr pavilion, one of the most memorable

buildings of the 1930s. Bexhill Central station, seen on 29 May 2000, was a spectacular response by the LBSCR to the threat posed by a rival line recently opened by the SE&CR.

Below: Bexhill boasted the usual Brighton lantern above the booking hall, which is similar to the better known lantern at Eastbourne. Long sloping ramps led down to the platforms. The LBSCR hoped that the spectacular growth that had taken place in the 1890s would continue, and planned on a grand scale, with a station that could accommodate vast crowds. As the 7th and 8th Earls de la Warr saw the town as a prestigious resort for the better class of holidaymaker, the LBSCR plan to cater for the masses may not have been what their lordships wished, but gave Bexhill station a spaciousness lacking from most stations. The town never grew as the LBSCR had hoped, and the size of the station became an embarrassment to British Rail and its successors, as it gradually decayed, as is sadly apparent from this study dating from May 2000. The station had received a Grade II

listing on 19 November 1999, because of the threat to its survival, if it deteriorated further. In September 2003, Bexhill Council served a notice under the Town & Country Planning Act 1990, on Network Rail and South Central Trains requiring specified repairs. This prompted a meeting and a refurbishment plan, commencing with the interior of the booking hall. Given Bexhill's fascinating architecture, of a late Victorian and Edwardian seaside town with one of the premier Art Deco buildings in the world, it is important that this spectacular Edwardian station should be a fitting ornament to the town. The 7th Earl de la Warr, who started Bexhill on this path, was a complex character, who succeeded to the title in 1873. He was a supporter of the Amalgamated Society of Railway Servants, and a fierce critic of the safety record of the railway companies in the House of Lords, yet when he turned Bexhill into a seaside resort, he wanted a genteel fashionable resort for the upper and middle classes, and insisted that vulgar shops and trades people should be kept remote from his end of the town.

Above: The Caledonian Railway engaged in a deadly rivalry with the Glasgow & South Western Railway on the south bank of the Clyde, taking commuters and holidaymakers between the centre of Glasgow and the residential towns and resorts on the Clyde Estuary. Wemyss Bay, a few miles south of where the Clyde turns south, was the most southerly Caledonian outpost on the Clyde, serving the steamers to the lovely Isle of Bute and other destinations. The station had been built in 1865, but the burgeoning growth of Glasgow in the closing decades of the Nineteenth century meant that residential and holiday traffic had overtaxed the station by 1900. Donald Alexander Matheson had been appointed engineer-in-chief of the Caledonian

Railway in 1899, and in conjunction with a brilliant architect, James Miller, developed proposals to rebuild the station to suit the level of traffic it was now facing. We have already encountered Miller on the West Highland Railway in 1894. He had been born at Auchtergaven in 1860 and educated at the Perth Academy where he and Matheson became school friends. Both worked in the CR engineers' office for some time, before Miller set up in independent practice in 1892. Although competitive tenders were invited for some Caledonian contracts, Matheson's influence ensured that all major CR work after he became Chief Engineer in 1899 went to Miller. For Wemyss Bay, Miller used the 'Domestic Revival' style for the frontage of the

new Wemyss Bay station in 1903, characterised by a profusion of steeply pitched half-timbered gables topping rendered walls on a mellow red sandstone footing. The concave treatment of the gables echoes the concave roof profile used on the West Highland stations in 1894, and the half timbering has many points in common. The station, which is often regarded as Matheson and Miller's finest work, became a Grade B listed structure, later accorded the rare accolade of being advanced to category A, a distinction usually only accorded to the most exceptional structures. It underwent a major refurbishment in 1993–94, and we see it a year later.

Below: Matheson was an innovate engineer and had noted the way that crowds tended to spread like flowing water, and how they were impeded by sharp corners and projections. The station was on a cramped site between the main road and the Clyde, swinging round sharply on to the pier, from which the Caledonian Steam Packet steamers departed. Matheson used this site to advantage, providing broad platforms and long graceful canopies, and on a site where many engineers would have provided an additional track at the expense of congested platforms, made platform 1 and 2 exceptionally broad, the left hand line being served from both sides of the track. As rapid embarking and disembarking of large crowds of commuters or holidaymakers was the goal. Matheson was undoubtedly correct in following what might be seen as a wasteful or unusual policy. The station roof was extensively glazed, as Matheson believed in a light airy appearance, the succession of arches curving into the distance being one of its most outstanding features.

Matheson had been born at Perth in 1860, and had attended the Perth Academy, where he met James Miller, and was later at Heriot Watt College in Edinburgh. After a spell on the LNWR, he became Engineer-in-Chief of the Caledonian Railway in 1899. In 1910, he made the unusual transition from engineer to General Manager, becoming General Manager, Scotland on the formation of the LMS in 1923, and retiring three years later.

Above: Matheson's genius in creating light open spaces with graceful curves was evident on the concourse, where the roof supports radiated out like spokes from a centrally positioned booking office. As with the main station buildings, which provided the circumference of the concourse, the lower part of the walls consisted of dressed pink sandstone blocks. This ingenious design minimised the number of columns required in the circulating area, and the sweeping curves channelled the crowds in the right direction. A few moments' study will reveal the careful positioning of the two columns in this view, crowds being naturally deflected to the left or right by the columns and the booking office, depending on which platform they are heading for. I do not think Donald Matheson would have regarded the awkward modern railing to the right of the view with great favour, this being one of the very few adverse features at an otherwise superbly restored station for which the Scottish Region of BR deserved great credit. In many ways, the use of sweeping curves at Wemyss Bay provided a blueprint for the much more ambitious reconstruction of Glasgow Central station a few years later. In both stations, Matheson achieved

a well-glazed circulating area that was free of intermediate columns and with projections and awkward corners swept away, contributed to good passenger flow.

Below: Our final view of this magnificent station shows what it was all about, as it is taken from one of the CalMac Steamers en route to Rothesay on the Isle of Bute. On the right, we see Miller's tall Italianate Domestic Revival clock tower, an unusual but successful blending of two very different architectural styles. To the left is the end gable of Miller's main station building with its half timbered mock Tudor gable. The curving structure in the foreground is the covered passage way from the station concourse to the steamer berths, which is

flanked at the seaward end by two diminutive Japanese pagoda towers in the so called Glasgow Movement style. The glazing for the circulating area rises up behind the covered passageway, and the curved wall supporting the canopy over platform No 1 stretches out in the distance on the left. Miller, who died in 1947, is recalled as a reserved man, who was deeply distressed when his only son, George, who had joined his father in the architectural practice, died in 1940, Miller retiring from work himself within a few months. With the influential backing of Matheson, he received virtually every major railway contract for the Caledonian Railway for twenty years, which was then at the height of its powers, and this success caused some professional jealousy.

Above: Hulme End, in the beautiful Manifold valley, was the northern terminus of one of the most exotic railways ever built in the British Isles. The Light Railways Act 1896 was a parliamentary response to the realisation that British agriculture was suffering from foreign competition, but the immense costs of an Act of Parliament and of complying with BoT regulations made any attempt to serve remote rural areas uneconomic. The Act replaced the costly private act of parliament with a cheap and simple public enquiry, and removed many of the BoT requirements that were appropriate to a busy main line, but over the top for a country branch with 3 or 4 trains a day. The Leek, Caldon Low and Hartington Light Railways order of 1898 approved four sections of line, one of which was to be narrow gauge. This would run from Waterhouses for 8 miles through the Manifold valley to Hulme End. It would be built to 2ft 6ins gauge, and when the original engineer died, E R Calthrop replaced him in December 1900. Calthrop had been born in 1857, and trained at Crewe, joining the GWR and then the Great Indian Peninsular Railway. He developed an interest in economical light railways, publishing a book on this theme, which culminated in a concession to build the 2 ft 6 ins gauge Barsi Light Railway in India, which opened in 1897. Calthrop applied

many of the ideas from Barsi in creating a railway in the Peak District of England, its two engines even sporting enormous headlamps and double tropical roofs. Construction began in 1902, and the line opened on 27 June 1904. Although constructed by a separate company, the Leek & Manifold Light Railway, the line was worked by the North Staffordshire Railway, so was absorbed into the LMS in 1923. Although the 1896 Act reduced construction costs, many lines were built in areas that could hardly support any railway even before motor competition, and by the 1930s, were suffering. The LMS decided enough was enough, closing the L&MVLR in March 1934. Hulme End station became a County Council Highways Depot, the station being used as offices and a store. We see the buildings in July 1991. The sloping awning that once projected out over the platform has gone, but otherwise the building had hardly altered in the decades since the last train clattered over Manifold metals. Staffordshire Moorlands District Council subsequently restored the station building as a visitors centre, incorporating a replacement canopy.

Left: Everard Richard Calthrop, who took up an interest in aviation in later life, and was also a keen horseman, would have been distressed to have seen the Manifold fall on hard times, but had passed away in 1927. A century after the L&MVLR opened, the corrugated iron loco shed he provided at Hulme End still survived, and although roller shutters had replaced the original wooden doors, the change was not too obtrusive and the structure could have been restored to its original form without undue difficulty. We see the shed in 1991 when still in use by the Highways Department. When Elena and I first visited Hulme End, and admired the progress on the restored station building, I

looked at the old loco shed, and hoped it too would receive attention, for the survival of these buildings seventy years after the railway last ran was miraculous. Tragically it was not to be. In 2006, there was sad news, for the loco shed that had survived for so many years in the hands of the Highways Department, was demolished, and a new structure put up in its place. There is a need with any structure for repairs, which can be extensive. However, the Staffordshire Moorlands District Council statement that the demolition of a surviving original structure counts as 'restoration' is bizarre. It would be akin to applauding the demolition of Westminster Abbey to build a replica, or painting a new Mona Lisa and throwing the old one in the fire. The Council, whose motto is 'Aiming for Excellence' did an excellent job on the station building for which they deserve praise. 'Aiming for Vandalism' might be a better motto for their conduct over the loco shed in 2006. Someone with a rich sense of irony corrected an absurd Council sign at Hulme End that claimed the work was 'restoration' to read 'vandalism'. They got it right. Sadly, it will not bring back a building that was one of the few relics of a fascinating Light Railway.

Above: In the early 1900s, a steam railcar craze swept the British Isles. The idea of a lightweight train to cater for branch line or inner suburban traffic economically and call at wayside halts to generate new traffic was sound, but most steam railcars were too unreliable or too under-powered, and wage costs were not significantly altered. The train might be small, but still required a driver, fireman and guard on full pay. If the railcar was small enough to offer worthwhile savings, it had to have little surplus capacity, which meant that it could not cope on market days and other peak periods. The

solutions were a larger railcar, which eroded the savings, or to run a conventional steam train, which meant a duplication of equipment. Most steam railcars were discarded within a few years, but there were three exceptions. The GWR, the LYR and the LNWR all built successful and long-lived designs, the last LY and LNWR cars being inherited by BR in 1948. One line to receive steam railcars was the cross-country route from Oxford to Bletchley and Cambridge. Several railcar halts were opened between Oxford and Bicester, and between Bletchley and Bedford, on 30 October 1905. The village of Bow Brickhill lay between Fenny Stratford and Woburn Sands, and a halt was provided to serve the village where the line crossed over a minor road. Compared with Morcott, which had been opened in 1898 (see page 58), with its up market version of the LNWR shed, Bow Brickhill received the basic hut with vertical boarding and shallow windows, together with a short timber platform. Although many of the Bletchley–Bedford stations were signalled from open-air ground frames, the LNWR had developed a simple signalling hut. This provided cover for shunt frames, and where the signalling requirements were confined to up and down distant and home signals, and gate controls, the crude lug locking of these ground frames was sufficient. Bow Brickhill boasted one of these diminutive signal huts, as we see in this view taken on 7 April 1967. The LNWR had taken the basic railway concept to the limit, but for the village it meant a frequent service of trains instead of a long walk to the nearest proper station.

Below: Seaside resorts are popular with modellers, as they have plenty of operating potential, and are often in an attractive location. Morecambe Promenade, which was opened at the height of the Edwardian era, was one of the finest. The 'Little' North Western Railway (NWR), then an independent company, which was building a line from Skipton to the Lancaster & Carlisle Railway, took over the powers of the Morecambe Bay & Harbour Co, and opened a short line between Lancaster and Poulton, as the station was initially named, on Whit Monday, 12 June 1848. The original terminus at the harbour was only used briefly, Morecambe Town station replacing it in 1851. By the turn of the century, holiday traffic to Morecambe had grown out of all belief, and the creation of an Irish Sea port at Heysham required upgrading of the Midland line most of the way to Morecambe. The Midland took the logical decision of also providing a new station at Morecambe, which was located on the promenade. The new station opened on 24 March 1907. By this time, the Midland had also decided to electrify the Lancaster – Morecambe –Heysham lines to get experience of electric traction, and although there was insufficient time to institute electric services when Morecambe Promenade station opened, this

took place the following year. The station buildings were constructed in a restrained Gothic style using a warm golden-honey stone to the designs of Thomas Wheatley. A dormer clock was provided in front of the central entrance with a porte cochere. We see this delightful frontage in July 1985, with a taxi drawn up beneath the canopy as the architect had intended. The shallow scalloped valance to the canopy matches the stone cornice.

Opposite top: A well-lit circulating area with a pitched roof led onto the platforms. With plenty of glazing, the light honey coloured stone and ivy bedecking the walls, the station was a perfect introduction to a holiday beside the seaside, and until the 1960s saw prodigious crowds, but this was not to last. The 1963 Beeching Report noted that BR passenger traffic in July 1961 exceeded winter levels by 47%, so that extra rolling stock had to be retained to cover this peak demand. Out of the 18,500 gangwayed coaches used on fast and semi-fast services in 1959, 6000 saw service not more than 18 times that year. Providing this stock cost £3.4m for net earnings of £0.5m. Beeching warned that this added to the BR deficit, concluding, 'Since the beginning of 1959 the number of passenger-carrying gangway coaches

has been reduced by 5,584 and at the end of 1965 stock will not be available for use at high peak periods. Efforts will be made to control these peaks by seat reservation schemes and by fares policy.' With BR hostile to the summer Saturday traffic, a long decline began, aided by the growth of cheap foreign holidays. As late as 1985, the station was still well used, and with its Grade II listed status, it was hoped that this would protect it. However, many seaside stations had been drastically downsized or even sold off, trains terminating further out, so that a prime development site could be released, and Morecambe Promenade station was closed in 1994, a new two platform station replacing it. As a listed building, it could not be demolished, so has survived as a restaurant, arts centre and tourist information centre.

Opposite bottom: Four long platforms, capable of handling full-length excursion trains, were provided. All were provided with escape crossovers, platforms 2 and 3 having a centre engine escape line, a feature normally only encountered at the busiest of termini. A fan of carriage sidings was provided to the left of the station, and motive power facilities included a large turntable for express passenger locomotives. Many of the holidaymakers who

flocked to Morecambe in the 1930s crossed the road to the Midland Hotel, which is visible to the right of the station. As Britain began to recover from the worst effects of the Wall St crash and the depression at the end of the twenties, British holiday resorts began to regain business, and Morecambe Corporation started revamping the promenade. The Midland Railway had opened a hotel facing the station, but in 1932, the LMS decided to create a

modern hotel to international quality. The company selected Oliver Hill as architect. He had an international reputation in modern hotel building and construction, and created the first Art Deco hotel in Britain. Because Art Deco buildings are rare in the British Isles, as the style, which evolved from the Bauhaus ideals, never became widely popular, it is the only Art Deco hotel to survive in the UK. Most Art Deco commissions were for houses or

apartments. As soon as it opened in July 1933, the Midland Hotel became the fashionable place to stay, and attracted the wealthy middle classes from the North of England. During World War Two, it was used as a hospital, being returned to the LMS in 1946. Later sold out of railway ownership, it declined in prestige, and although listed on account of its historic importance, was badly neglected for many years, but a restoration project hopes to see it refurbished.

Below: With thousands of holidaymakers arriving from Yorkshire on Summer Saturdays, the town gained the nickname, 'Bradford-by-the-Sea'. Rapid clearance of these excursion trains was essential, so large double gates were provided at each end of the building, which could be opened at peak periods. An imposing gateway, that would have done justice to a cathedral or a baronial hall, with a four centred arch that epitomised the ecclesiastical connotations of high Victorian gothic was topped by a shield bearing the MR monogram.

Elsewhere, pointed arch windows and quatrefoils reinforced this image, and the result, in a seaside town lacking urban pollution was superb. It also constituted a glorious swansong for Victorian railway gothic, as architectural tastes were changing, and the station, though a treasure, was regarded as somewhat dated.

Bottom: Although modellers may not want to build Morecambe, the station offers ideas for a layout, so I am portraying the station approach from platform 3. This reveals the overbridge at the station throat, followed by a sharp double reverse curve, with the tracks fanning out to serve the four platforms, the loco escape line between platforms 2 and 3, run round tracks for platforms 1 and 4 and the carriage sidings to the right. The station is controlled from a Midland Railway signal box, partly visible on the right. For the modeller, who is short of space, the reverse curve could be replaced by a continuous curve, to an L shape, but the overbridge is a perfect scenic break. Placing the station approach tracks at an angle to the platforms, as at Morecambe, makes a useful saving in space, and creates a more attractive station, but is seldom seen in model form.

Opposite top: The GWR had slumbered in the latter part of the nineteenth century, but with the elimination of the broad gauge, came a reawakening, and just as the GWR had blazed a trail in the 1830s and 1840s, the company made the two decades between the end of the Broad gauge in 1892 and the outbreak of World War I in 1914 a period of sustained development. The way in which G J Churchward transformed locomotive practice is well known, but James Inglis, the GWR engineer who became general manager, finally rid the company of the epithet, the Great Way Round, with a series of cut-offs that shortened mileage between major centres. The Badminton Direct line and the creation of the GW & GC line and of the Aynho cut-off are the most dramatic, but the 'North Warwicks' was another crucial line, that owed its origins to dissatisfaction with GWR services south of Birmingham. It had been authorised as an independent company in 1894 to run from a new terminus at Moor St in Birmingham to Stratford. After a flirtation with the GCR, which ended when the GWR offered a better deal to the GC, the North Warwicks line was amended to join the GWR at Tyseley. However, the idea of a Moor St terminus for suburban trains appealed to the GWR, as Snow Hill station was already overtaxed. The southern end of the line was also revised to join the existing GWR route to Stratford at Bearley. The 'North Warwicks' opened to freight in December 1907, and to passengers on 1 July 1908. Although a suburban railway, it was engineered to main line standards, as the GWR saw it as a link in a new Birmingham to Bristol main line to eclipse the Midland route, as it was not hampered by the formidable 1 in 37 Lickey incline. In this portrait, from the Up platform at Henley in Arden on 2 August 1971, we see a turn-of-the-century GWR main line little altered in over sixty years. On the left is a characteristic water crane and drain funnel that so typified the GWR. The lower quadrant platform starter, with its ball and spike finial is pure 'Reading', the GWR signal works being at Reading. The upper quadrant down home signal near the box is a modern replacement, based on LMS practice, but the box is a standard GWR type 7d box, in bright red brick with blue Staffordshire engineering brick footings and quoining, i.e. the alternate short and long blue bricks at the corners of the buildings, and around the door frame. The box dates from the opening of the line in 1907.

Below: Henley-in-Arden, pop 3,000, should not be confused with Henley-on-Thames, which was also on the GWR. Leaving Birmingham, the North Warwicks line served the developing commuter belt around Hall Green and Shirley, and the GWR had hopes that Henley, which was just over half way to Stratford, would also develop as a commuter town, but this was never fulfilled on the scale Paddington had hoped for. Impressive buildings were provided on both platforms and a bay platform was provided for terminating trains from Birmingham to the left, the track leading to the platform being visible in the previous view. The Badminton 1902 style buildings appeared in two main variants. One version, which is illustrated in the introduction, (page 4) was provided with a hipped roof and a separate canopy projecting over the platform. In the second version, the building was flat-roofed, the canopy sheltering the building, as well as the platform. Henley was built to this pattern. In modern times, many buildings of this type have lost their canopies, leaving a flat-roofed structure lacking charm. The GWR lattice footbridge with monogram in the triangular plate supporting the second rise of steps is well known, but in the early 1900s, a plate girder design was adopted, as at Henley.

Top: Because of the heavy traffic on the main line out of Euston, the LNWR was reluctant to encourage short haul commuter traffic, but with residential development, there was a 200% increase in traffic between Watford and London from 1884 to 1904. At the August 1906 stockholders general meeting, plans were revealed for a new electrified line that would parallel the main line as far as Bushey, where it would loop to the west to serve the centre of Watford, before terminating at Watford Junction. The new lines were brought into use in stages in 1912-1913, the section from Harrow to Watford being opened on 10 February 1913. The lines were initially steam worked, electrification having taken longer to develop

than expected, and being introduced between 1914 and 1917. Hatch End station was the work of Gerald Horsley (1862–1917). Horsley came from a talented family, one brother being a well-known painter, another a leading surgeon. His father was John Calcott Horsley RA (1817–1903), whilst his grandfather and great grandfather were both talented composers. There was also a railway connection through his Aunt Mary, who was married to Isambard Kingdom Brunel. At Hatch End, Gerald Horsley used a combination of red brick with white terracotta banding, or string courses, on the Neo-Georgian entrance pavilion, and at platform level. The pavilion was rectangular with a pyramid roof, topped with a clock tower,

cupola and weathervane. We are looking towards Watford in 1978.

Above: At a station such as Hatch End, where there was a separate high level entrance and platform level buildings, the latter were often in the standard railway house style, but Gerald Horsley was able to impart individuality to the structure, with an impressive and imaginative roof line and strong verticals. This was not surprising, given Horsley's artistic family background. He had trained under the legendary Richard Norman Shaw (1831–1912), and with four other young trainees, had formed St George's Art Society in 1883 to discuss the growing split between art and architecture. The

following year, Horsley joined another group known as 'The Fifteen', to form the Art Workers' Guild, where designers, artists, architects and craftsmen met to discuss their crafts and learn from one another. Their goal was to reunite art and architecture, and their ideas became a potent force in the move from Victorian Gothic to newer styles.

Top: The Light Railways Act 1896 had been intended to encourage the construction of agricultural railways, but many Light Railway orders related to tramways, or to conventional railways. The Derwent Valley Light Railway was one of the few genuine agricultural railways created as a result of the act. It opened from Wheldrake to Cliff Common in 1912, and to York (Layerthorpe) in 1913, making connections with the NER at both ends. A limited passenger service ran until 1926, but its primary purpose was to handle farm traffic. The line was not merged into the Big Four in 1923, and miraculously escaped nationalisation in 1948. When BR closed the former NER line through Cliff Common, the DVLR lost its southern connection, and the line was cut back to Wheldrake in 1965, and to Dunnington by 1973. Although passenger services had ceased in 1926, the station buildings at Dunnington survived when I visited the station on 9 July 1974. To cut costs, they were of wooden chalet construction with half-timbering that had been painted in contrasting colours at one time. The roof was clad with diamond tiles. Hatch End and Dunnington both opened in the same year, but the contrast between a busy suburban railway on a passenger-only line and an agricultural light railway could hardly be more dramatic. This diversity was one of the charms of the railway network that existed not so many years ago. The wagon in the platform, 7592, is one of the celebrated 'blues' operated by the British Railway Traffic & Electric Co, or BRT, a wagon hire firm. It is a 37 ton glw grain hopper

to a design introduced in 1965, and was operated to the Yorkshire Grain Dryers plant at Dunnington, which was the mainstay of traffic by the mid-seventies.

Below: The YGD plant at Dunnington had been established through the initiative of James Acklam, the long serving manager of the DVLR. Realising that general agricultural business was collapsing, Acklam offered long term leases of surplus DVLR land at Dunnington to YGD, who used the line until 1981. A tourist steam passenger service ran from 1976 to 1979, but was unprofitable. Following Acklam's retirement, the heart seemed to go out of the

DVLR, and although York Layerthorpe station survived for a while as an oil terminal, this ended, and the station sites were sold for property development. A short section of line was opened as a preserved railway in the vicinity of the one time Murton station between Layerthorpe and Dunnington in 1993. In this view, taken at Dunnington on 9 July 1974, we are looking towards the station buildings in the distance. The YGD plant is on the left, with the YGD 0-4-0DM shunter, *Churchill,* which was built by John Fowler in 1947. The former running line to Cliff Common is on the right, but is now a dead end siding, and is occupied by BRT grain hoppers.

Top: About the time that Donald Matheson made the transition from Engineer-in-Chief of the Caledonian Railway to General Manager in 1910, he took a holiday in the magnificent countryside between Perth and Stirling. He was enchanted with the beauty of Glen Eagles, and having visited the United States in 1902, was aware that many US Railroads developed resorts to bring traffic to their systems. This was an unusual idea for the British Isles, but Matheson decided that a premier hotel would bring prestige and business to the Caledonian Railway. The result was the Gleneagles hotel. The Caledonian board approved the construction of a new station and golf course at a cost of £20,000 in 1913, but because of the war, it was not until 1919 that the station and golf course were ready. Matheson followed progress on the hotel with keen interest, but for the same reason this was not completed until 1924. Golfing holidays were becoming popular, and Matheson hired one of the leading golfers of the day, James Braid, to lay out two exceptional courses, which have made

Gleneagles a magnet for golfers for over eighty years. To cater for the business that his hotel and golf course would generate, Matheson decided that Crieff Junction station would be rebuilt on a lavish scale, and renamed Gleneagles. His old school friend and colleague in rebuilding Wemyss Bay and Glasgow Central, James Miller, was appointed architect, and the station, in a mellow Edwardian Domestic style, was graced with the usual Matheson/Miller hallmarks of wide platforms, broad canopies and superb woodwork.

Below: Although the Gleneagles hotel was not ready until 1924, work on the station was well advanced, and the rebuilt station was completed in 1919. The world had just emerged from a traumatic war, and the commemorative stone said simply, 'BUILT IN 1919 THE YEAR OF THE PEACE AFTER THE GREAT WAR'. The station is a listed Grade B structure. Although Miller had prepared the initial designs for the station and hotel, completion of the project in 1919 was in the

hands of the CR architect, Matthew Adam. With the golf course also opening in 1919, it was not long before Matheson's ambitious plans started to pay off. In 1921, a forerunner of what would eventually become the Ryder Cup was held over the King's course, when a ten-man British side defeated a strong US team decisively. In later years, Bob Hope, the legendary US comedian, and a talented golfer, was to become a regular visitor to Gleneagles.

Opposite top: At Gleneagles station, a broad footbridge connected the two main platforms, the footbridge towers being of rendered construction and graced with bay windows, an unusual touch that added rare distinction and charm to this already impressive station. James Miller, whose working career in Glasgow spanned half a century, had specialised in railway work in his early days, but after winning competitions for the design of the Glasgow Royal Infirmary and the Glasgow International Exhibition in 1901, his fame spread. Although much of his time after 1900 was spent on prestige hotels, he remained happy to work with Matheson. As Donald Matheson sought an international clientele, which meant looking to the growing affluence of the United States, and Miller had been keenly interested in the ideas Matheson had brought back from a 1902 visit to the States, his selection for Gleneagles was ideal. A mild American idiom had appeared in Miller's work as early as 1898, but within months of Matheson returning from the US trip, a much stronger American influence was

apparent, with the construction of the Olympia House in Queen Street, Glasgow in 1903. This echoed contemporary American frame buildings, with a high-level colonnade that became popular in America in the 1890s. These crosscurrents, with a senior railway engineer influencing the style of one of Scotland's premier architects is remarkable evidence of the power and prestige of the Caledonian Railway in the early 1900s. Although completion of the hotel was placed in Matthew Adam's hands, to Miller's disappointment, the hotel was imbued with Miller's transatlantic style.

Below: The bay windows, a most unusual idea to incorporate in footbridge towers, showed how innovative Matheson and Miller could be. Their combined talents served the Caledonian Railway well and gave a turn-of-the-century boost to an already impressive collection of railway buildings in Scotland. Sadly, because Scotland's railways have tended to be neglected by railway writers, these architectural gems are seldom fully appreciated.

NEW NAMES, NEW PROBLEMS
1923–1939

The Great War of 1914–18 had wrought unimaginable social, economic, technological and political changes in society. On the political side, parliament changed from resolute opposition to any mergers between the bigger companies to imposing a shotgun marriage that reduced over 100 companies to just four. Much of Ireland went its own way, separate from the United Kingdom. Wage costs had rocketed, and union power was greater than ever before, and pressure mounted to cut costs. Road vehicles had developed rapidly due to the stimulus of war. New styles were appearing in architecture. How the railways coped with all these issues, and the impact of this myriad of factors on stations, is the subject of this section.

Above: The Fylde Coast owes its popularity to the determination of Sir Peter Hesketh Fleetwood, who turned the desolate Fylde into a string of popular residential communities, holiday resorts and a port between 1840 and 1900. The 7.5 mile long Blackpool & Lytham Railway, which was isolated from the rest of the railway network, was incorporated in 1861, opening two years later. It was taken over jointly by the LNWR and LYR in 1871, and powers were obtained to convert it into a through route. The resort of St Anne's-on-the-

Sea did not then exist, the first station in the vicinity, which was named Cross Slack, opened in 1873, and assumed the name St Anne's in January 1875. By 1920, traffic to the Fylde had mushroomed. Whilst Blackpool catered for the mass market, St Anne's had a fashionable following. This was not unusual in holiday areas. In the Isle of Man, Douglas catered for the mass market, whilst Ramsey catered for the more affluent visitor. Major improvements were planned by the LNWR and LYR for St Anne's, with the platforms to be lengthened by 50%, and a new building to replace the original 1871 structure on the down side of the line. With the grouping, work commenced under LMS auspices in 1923, with the station well advanced for the start of the 1924 summer season, an LMS estimate of £38,686 covering work for that year. Further minor expenditure in 1925/26 completed a well thought out and spacious station well-suited to peak holiday crowds. We see the station approach road and road frontage in 1981.

Opposite bottom: We are looking from the down platform towards Blackpool in 1981. Freight services had ended in November 1968, but the station had otherwise changed little in the decades since it was built. Sadly this once important main line was singled in 1985 as a part of the retreat from serving the holiday

summer Saturday peak traffic. The reduction of the station to a single platform destroyed the charm and symmetry of this attractive early post-grouping station. In the previous section, we looked at Donald Matheson's superb station at Wemyss Bay, with its broad platforms and generous exits. St Anne's was another station that had to handle heavy holiday traffic, and the same generous provision of broad and uncluttered platforms and plenty of exits was evident. Unfortunately, the demise of the Summer Saturday holiday traffic, foreshadowed in the Beeching Report of 1963, dealt a deathblow to stations such as St Anne's, although the rise of overseas package holidays and universal car ownership would have eventually achieved a similar result, even without the Beeching policy of pricing the traffic off rail as being uneconomic.

Below: The London Transport surface lines offer many interesting features for the modeller that could be transposed to a different setting. This is particularly the case with the former Metropolitan Railway, as the 'Met' once entertained main line ambitions, with a main line that ran from Baker Street to Verney Junction. Croxley is the sole intermediate station on the short branch that diverged from the main line south of Rickmansworth, and ran for two miles to Watford. It was built during the

long and distinguished reign of R H Selbie as general manager of the Met, and was constructed jointly with the LNER, opening on 2 November 1925, and was part of the 'Metroland' image promoted so energetically by the company. Originally named Croxley Green (as the station is in Croxley Green), it was renamed Croxley on 23 May 1949 to avoid confusion with the terminus of the former LNWR branch from Watford. The booking office and adjacent road were carried over the line on a series of plate girders, the platform facilities being confined to waiting shelters. Once again, it is a design that would provide an excellent scenic break for the modeller. The fairy lights festooned from the lampposts are not a Christmas decoration, as this illustration was taken on 14 August 1989, but alternative lighting during an upgrade to the antiquated but elegant lighting system. Services were suspended on the nearby LNWR branch from Watford to Croxley Green in 1996, and proposals were approved in 2005 to divert the Metropolitan Watford branch north of Croxley to join the disused LNWR line to Watford Junction. A view of the road elevation of Croxley station, which handled some 600,000 passengers per annum, appears on the rear cover.

Above: Herbert Ashcombe Walker was a highly respected LNWR officer, but became general manager of the London & South Western Railway in 1912. He headed the electrification of the LSWR suburban lines from 1915, and when the SR was formed, was the obvious candidate to take over. He realised that the company had a poor image, and responded with smarter working, electrification, and good PR. The competition between the SER and LCDR had led to some awkward lines around Margate and Ramsgate, and a new station on a chord that connected these former rivals replaced the cramped SER and LCDR stations in

Ramsgate. The new lines were opened on 2 July 1926. Built on a green field site, there was space for a lavish station and an electric stock depot. The new lines were the work of the Chief Engineer, A W Szlumper, (1858-1934). He had trained under his elder brother, James, and after working in South Wales, on the SER and in India, joined the LSWR in 1884, becoming chief engineer in 1914. Major works included the rebuilding of Waterloo station, and the enlargement of Southampton docks, the Ramsgate project of 1926 being one of his last jobs before retiring in 1927. The dominant feature at Ramsgate was a palatial booking hall,

with a vaulted ceiling with modernist mouldings, the end walls having an Egyptian theme, this being popular due to the discoveries made in the Valley of the Kings in the 1920s. Three massive round-topped windows illuminated the booking hall. The top of the arches is particularly dramatic, whilst the barley twist moulding on the brick surround to the windows adds detail, without being fussy.

Below: The architect seems to have been Edwin Fry, who designed some of the finest 'New Classical' buildings of this era. Edwin Maxwell Fry, who was born on 2 August 1899 and died on 3 September 1987, was trained at the School of Architecture at the University of Liverpool, and was one of the few modernist architects working in Britain in the thirties who was British; most having fled Nazi persecution, where the Bauhaus ideals were abhorred. Although many modernist architects had socialist views, Fry had traditional patriarchal values, believing that professional middle class architects should create a better environment for the less fortunate, and much of his work was directed towards improved housing for the poor. The exterior with its keystones and shaped mouldings stressed the Egyptian theme. The LMS station at St Anne's was excellent, but Szlumper and Fry put the Southern in premier position with Ramsgate and Margate. Just as Victorian architecture was reviled in the 1920s, Fry's New Classical style was not appreciated for many years, and this station, which is now seen as probably the finest New Classical railway building in the British Isles, was not granted Listed Grade II status until 1988.

Right: A 'new' date can usually be assigned to a station, but modification and enlargement ensues, and unless the old station is replaced, or a new station built on a new site, the result may well be a station that contains elements from the day it was built to recent weeks or even days. Some stations such as Gleneagles or St Anne's-on-the-Sea, which owed little to their predecessors, are easy to date, whilst Ramsgate was on a new site, but others are problematical. Few offer greater challenges than Newport (Mon). The station was built for the South Wales Railway in 1848–50, but drastically rebuilt by the GWR in 1875–78, just a small portion of the original station surviving. In 1928, the GWR carried out major work, so should the station be dated as 1848, 1878 or 1928? We could split the coverage amongst these periods, but at Newport, the station is so intermingled that this is not helpful. As the dominant influence is given by the 1928 rebuilding, I have explored it here. As with many large GWR stations, there are two through roads flanked by the up and down platforms. We are looking from the up platform, No 2, towards and Paddington in June 1994. Apart from the four through tracks visible, two further through roads existed on the left. The five-story red brick block on the right is the 1928 office block that housed station facilities, and the divisional offices that had grown due to the grouping and the acquisition of the previously independent South Wales valleys railways. The footbridge tower, with its older stonework and round headed windows, is a part of the 1878 station, which was the work of Lancaster Owen and J R Danks. The buildings on the up platform on the left are part of the

Owen/Danks rebuild that followed the style of the original station. The tapered columns and lattice framework, with curved gussets where the members join, is typical of canopy renewals between the wars at large GWR stations.

Below: The Up platform at Newport is separated by four tracks from the down platform No 1 on which we are standing. A further two tracks pass round the back of the up platform. The up building is a part of the 1878 work by Owen and Danks, but follows the style of the original 1848 station. When stone is used as a building material, many different finishes

can be adopted, from the precision of ashlar walling with smooth faced blocks of equal size, to the apparent chaos of random rubble, where rough hewn stone of any size is laid apparently randomly, but actually with considerable care by the stone mason. This is a rusticated or rock faced stone that has not been given the smooth surface of ashlar construction, but has been cut square or rectangular. The good lighting on the down platform means that it is possible to study not just the lattice girder that supports the canopy above our head, but the steel framework to which the decorative wooden valance is attached.

Above: It would be hard to imagine a bigger contrast between the busy station at Newport, with its five-story office block, and the sylvan setting of Penhelig, with its tiny wooden building with a pagoda shaped roof. We tend to see the period from 1923 to 1939 as one of slow decline, with a number of celebrated closures, such as the Leek & Manifold, or the Lynton & Barnstaple Light Railway, but the Big Four were also seeking ways of attracting new traffic, and this included opening many new halts. The GWR had developed the pagoda roof corrugated iron shelter at the turn of the century for minor wayside halts, constructing them into the 1930s, but at Penhelig, which is located a few yards south of Aberdovey No 4 tunnel, on the dramatic section where the Cambrian Coast line hugs the north bank of the Dovey Estuary between Dovey Junction and Aberdovey, the GWR provided a timber version of the pagoda with a felt covered roof. The station was opened on 8 May 1933, and was one of over twenty unstaffed halts opened by the GWR on the former Cambrian section between July 1923 and October 1939. These stations were request halts, and in many parts of the rail network, such halts have long gone, but Penhelig remains open at the time of writing. In the last year for which full figures were available, 2004-05, it is estimated that 8,795 passengers used the station, which is served by Arriva Trains Wales.

Below: The GWR Didcot–Oxford line crosses the Thames on Appleford Viaduct a short distance north of Didcot. For many years, the first station after leaving Didcot was Culham, which was provided with a superb Brunellian station building, which still survives. Apart from serving remote rural areas, the GWR also sited halts where they would serve new residential developments on the outskirts of towns, and a further group of halts opened in conjunction with the new diesel railcar services introduced in the mid-thirties, with their ability to stop and start away quickly from a minor wayside station. Appleford benefited from these trends, and received simple timber built platforms, made of old railway sleepers. Unlike Penhelig with its unusual timber pagoda, it received the standard corrugated iron Pagoda shelters, so called on account of the reversed curve on the roof that resembled a Chinese pagoda. The Pagoda had become quite widespread since the early 1900s, and on account of its distinctive shape, has always enjoyed popularity with modellers, but some halts were lacking in any shelter, whilst conventional buildings were also erected. As the next station to the north was Culham, with its venerable Brunellian buildings, the contrast could scarcely have been more pronounced, and shows how a line can develop over the years. The station is depicted looking north towards Oxford on 27 July 1989. Sadly, the two pagodas were removed in 2004, to be replaced by crude plywood shelters taking away a little more of the character of our railways.

Right: After completing the London–Bristol main line, and the Didcot–Oxford spur, the GWR looked towards the Midlands and the Mersey, the Birmingham & Oxford Junction Railway being proposed to carry broad gauge metals from Fenny Compton to Leamington Spa and Birmingham. The line opened to passengers on 1 October 1852. Leamington, a Regency spa town, was the only sizeable community between Banbury and Birmingham, and was in a hollow, the lines climbing steeply in both directions. For a major spa town, the GWR provided two through roads and two platform roads, all being covered by a classic Brunel timber trainshed. Within fifty years, this vast structure had succumbed to the ravages of locomotive exhaust, and was cut back to a stump, level with the platform edge. Even so, it was fragile, and between 1905 and 1911, the residual trainshed was cut back to the line of the columns embedded in the platform, and a sloping screen added. It was dreadful, and local irritation with this decaying station prompted the GWR architect, P E Culverhouse, to plan a replacement in the 1930s. The old forecourt had been at rail level, and in 1937, E C Jordan of Newport received a contract to excavate the forecourt down to road level. The residual Brunel trainshed and buildings were swept away, and Holliday & Greenwood erected a new steel framed structure, for £35,353. Brick infill, faced with dressed limestone blocks, created a station that blended the Regency theme of Leamington Spa with 1930s modernism. Even the stainless steel window frames blended, and the structure represents the summit of GWR architecture in the interwar years. Work was completed in 1939, and the forecourt and main block had altered little by 15 June 1971. The subway to the right gave access to the LNWR Leamington Spa Avenue station, which had closed in the 1960s, and to the town centre.

Below: As GWR architect for most of the Interwar period, Culverhouse moved the company from the Edwardian style of A H Webbe through 1920s Neo-Georgian to a dignified version of Art Deco. Gradual evolution is not as exciting as violent revolution, but often achieves a better result. Most of his stations, including Temple Meads and Paddington were alterations to an existing masterpiece, and Culverhouse achieved a contemporary look without violent conflict with the past. At Leamington, he had a clean slate, making the station of particular interest. A subway connected the main buildings on the down side with the up platform, the facilities comprising a single story brick building, a long canopy and a lift shaft. We are looking towards Birmingham, from the down platform on 15 June 1971. Although an important 1930s building, it was not listed until 2003, the impetus coming from local societies, rather than the local authorities. The community are to be congratulated on their determination, as the Grade 2 listing should hopefully prevent a repetition of the destruction wrought at Hastings in 2004, when the towns classical 1930s station with its remarkable octagonal booking hall was demolished as part of a redevelopment project.

Opposite top: In 1923, the LMS took over the Wirral Railway, which made an end on junction with the Mersey Railway at Birkenhead Park. The Mersey Railway, which tunnelled under the river to a low level terminus in Liverpool, had been electrified as early as 1903, but the Wirral could not afford to, so passengers used a Mersey train from Liverpool to Birkenhead Park, and then changed to a steam hauled Wirral train to continue their journey. In 1938, the LMS electrified the Wirral lines, instituting joint through working with the Mersey railway, and rebuilding many stations in the Wirral peninsula. The LMS had commissioned 'The Midland Hotel' at Morecambe in the Art Deco style in 1932, and the amazing public response convinced the LMS that Art Deco could also be applied to stations. New stations were provided for the Wirral electrification at Moreton, Meols, Leasowe and Hoylake, of which Hoylake was the best. The buildings were the work of the LMS Chief Engineer's office, but the LMS had an outstanding team in the 1930s, under the company's Chief Engineer William Kelly Wallace (1883–1969). He had joined the MR NCC on a permanent basis in 1906, and although a civil engineer, succeeded Bowman Malcolm when the latter retired in 1922, having been the Northern Counties locomotive engineer since 1876 and civil engineer since 1906. Wallace was promoted to Chief Stores Superintendent of the LMS in 1930, and Chief Civil Engineer in 1934. His team included the Architectural Assistant, W H Hamlyn, of Wigan. Hamlyn had redesigned Leeds station and the Queen's Hotel in Art Deco style between 1935 and 1937, and used similar ideas in the Wirral. A reinforced concrete

framework with brick filling provided a new image, as did the steel window frames in the characteristic 1930s shape. Canopies were of reinforced concrete, the supporting beams being above the canopy, leaving the underside uncluttered save for light fittings. At Hoylake, the most important station to be revamped, the frontage and the canopy curved out into the forecourt. The strong horizontal lines create an impression of speed.

Opposite bottom: An upper clerestory surmounted the main building, the sweeping curves of the ground floor being repeated at this level. As the line crossed a busy road, a concrete footbridge doubled as a station overbridge and a pedestrian crossing, with separate entrances from the street and the platform. When new, it must have been impressive, but by the 1970s, time had taken its toll of the concrete, which was stained and crumbling, as is apparent from this illustration. This was an inherent problem with many 1930s structures. If buildings were clad in limestone, or Portland stone, they remained smart. The brick infill in the Wirral was also robust, but structures entirely of concrete, such as footbridges, were prone to crumble, and if moisture percolated into the concrete to attack the steel reinforcing, the result was serious. With this caveat, the LMS had taken a dramatic step forward. In the 1920s, the LMS, the LNER and the GWR had produced competent new stations, but the Southern led the way with ambitious designs at Ramsgate or Margate. In 1937, the Southern built Surbiton in 'The Odeon Style'. Because of its location, Surbiton

is better known than Hoylake, but W H Hamlyn's use of prominent sweeping curves and his first floor circular clerestory at Hoylake means that this station must count as one of the finest Art Deco stations of the interwar years.

Above: From the footbridge, it was possible to see the reinforced concrete beams that support the cantilever roof. The immense weight of a cantilever roof would tip a building forward if there was not a balance weight at the rear. To make this unobtrusive, the counterweight was a massive concrete block at the rear of the building between ground level and platform level. At most of the rebuilt stations, where the buildings were set back ten feet from the platform edge, this was sufficient, but at Hoylake, the Down shelter, which is on the right, was set back 14 feet, which called for a balance wall of no less than 7ft 6ins deep which projected below ground level. The term Art Deco covers items from household ornaments to buildings and even the streamlined Gresley A4. The style flourished in the 20s and 30s, and was helped by the Paris Exhibition of 1925, and after the rise to power of Adolf Hitler in Germany in 1933, by the exodus of many Bauhaus and Art Deco designers, as their ideas were labelled degenerate by the Nazis. Art Deco embraced many themes, such as Cubism, with its zigzags and geometrical shapes, Egyptian, which followed the discovery of the tomb of Tutankhamun by Howard Carter and Lord Carnaervon in 1922, and the South American Aztec and Mayan school. New materials such as bakelite, an early form of plastic, stainless steel, chrome and aluminium were popular.

THE EFFECTS OF WAR

The outbreak of war in September 1939 resulted in most station improvements being put on hold for 'the duration'. In a few places wartime traffic necessitated new stations whilst the activity of the Luftwaffe called for remedial work as well.

Below: As Hitler's demands became ever more strident, the shadows of war lengthened, and plans were made to expand the motor and aero industries. Coventry, a motor town with a pool of skilled labour was an obvious place to do so. Apart from the factories, the workers required transport, and with the import of oil and rubber under threat from German U-boats, every effort was made to channel traffic on to the railways rather than buses. Canley Gates signal box controlled a level crossing west of Coventry on the London & Birmingham main line. A large Standard Motors plant was established on the

north side of the line, and the LMS opened a halt at the level crossing on 30 September 1940. Compared with the 1938 Art Deco station at Hoylake , Canley Halt was crude, with a small brick booking office with a sloping roof on the down platform, and a couple of plain shelters further along, but the pressures of war demanded a station using the least time and materials. It was usual for a station and an adjacent signal box to have the same name, and with the box called Canley Gates, the halt was spoken of by that title, although officially Canley Halt. Even the LMS got confused, with some official papers referring to Canley Gates (Halt). The end of the hostilities in 1945 saw many wartime facilities closed, but Canley was popular, and survived. When Coventry Power box was commissioned, Canley became a fringe box, and when the Coventry PSB area was extended to meet up with Phase 3 of New St PSB commissioning on 2–4 July 1966, Canley, Tile Hill and Berkswell were added to Coventry panel. We see the station on 19 March 1966, still with an old-fashioned oil lamp on the left, the LNWR signal box, and the basic station

building. Today, the location is unrecognisable, as the level crossing, the signal box and the buildings have all been replaced.

Bottom: The early postwar years were a time of austerity, when materials were rationed, and priority given to exports. Although the railways had suffered due to the blitz , they came down the queue for materials, so urgent projects were delayed. This contrasted with the continent, where the railways had suffered more damage, but were accorded a higher priority, and recovered faster than in the UK. At Derby, Robert Stephenson's trainshed, which dated from 1839–41, had stood for a century, and would probably have stood for many more years, had not a German bomb destroyed 100 yards of it in 1941. The wreckage was cleared to reopen the station, but the shed was not readily repairable, and the rest was removed in 1952. Individual concrete canopies were provided over each platform between 1952 and 1954. We see the 1950s canopies on 6 July 1976. The buildings include the 1839–1841 station designed by Francis Thompson.

DEVELOPMENTS SINCE 1948

British Railways was born because of political dogma, and died almost half a century later because of political dogma. Whether either decision was right is a moot point, but railwaymen had a job to do, and subject to ever growing political pressure, they did it to the best of their abilities. They had immense problems to contend with, including rapid inflation and growing competition from road vehicles. The loss of traditional traffics wrought havoc on railway finances, leading to the draconian cuts of the Beeching era, and the need to curtail costs everywhere. Thousands of old stations were closed; many more were reduced to basic halts, and a few new stations were built. In this section, we look at some of the highs, and the lows, of this remarkable period. One of the most interesting aspects of this period was the way that the existing architectural sections of the companies were transformed into regional architects under the overall control of Dr F F C Curtis whose long career spanned the transition of BR from a traditional steam worked system to the modern-image rail network that exists today.

Above: For the first station on this section, it is worth stepping back to the latter part of the nineteenth century. Albert Henry Stanley was born near Derby in 1874, and emigrated to the United States with his parents. He started out as an odd job man with the Detroit Street Railway, but his career represented the American Dream of rags to riches, as Stanley rose through the ranks of the Detroit Street Railway, which would be called a tramway in British parlance, becoming its general superintendent by the age of 28. Moving to the East coast, he was general manager of the Public Service Corporation of New Jersey at the age of 32 in 1907. US commercial backers dominated the evolution of London's underground lines at this time, and a few months later Stanley was sent to England as general manager of Underground Electric Railways Ltd, welding the Underground into a brilliantly led transport undertaking, that embraced underground railways, tramways and motor buses. He was to serve as President of the Board of Trade from 1916 to 1919, for which he received his peerage, as first Baron Ashfield of Southwell. Returning to the Underground, he became the first chairman of the London Passenger Transport Board on its formation in 1933. Under Lord Ashfield, the Underground group had pursued a policy of opening new lines ahead of residential development whilst land was cheap and readily available. The LT 'New Works Programme 1935-40' proposed to

extend the Central Line from North Acton to West Ruislip, running alongside the GWR Princes Risborough line. Lines that were well advanced when war broke out in 1939 were completed, but the West Ruislip extension was deferred for the duration. Construction resumed in 1946, the line reaching Greenford the following year. On 1 January 1948, the LPTB was absorbed into the British Transport Commission as the London Transport Executive, Ashfield becoming deputy chairman of the BTC. The West Ruislip section opened on 21 November 1948, the only remaining part of Ashfield's 1935 programme unfinished being the line to Epping in 1949. Sadly, Ashfield failed to see the last fruits of his vision, passing away on 4 November 1948. The design for West Ruislip station was prepared in 1946 by F F C Curtis, of the GWR, and later the Western Region, on behalf of LT. Because of postwar austerity, it was not completed until 1962, under the direction of Howard Cavanagh, but largely followed the Curtis plan, with a concave road frontage with sand coloured brickwork. The cantilevered concrete canopy with a fluted lower surface or soffit, was another Curtis feature, as was the pole-mounting of the Western Region 'totem', and the LT roundel.

Above: Whilst under Sir Edward William Watkin's rule, the MSLR and the Metropolitan Railway had enjoyed friendly relations, but subsequently they drifted apart, a problem not helped by the density of traffic on the Met Line, which obstructed GC expresses. The GC was moving closer to the GWR, which saw the benefits of a line striking north west out of London in shortening its existing but circuitous route to Birmingham. A joint line was agreed from Acton, south east of Ruislip, to Ashendon Junction, where GC trains diverged on to their own metals, GW trains continuing on another cut-off to Aynho. The new line, which utilised part of the old GWR branch between High Wycombe and Princes Risborough, opened on 2 April 1906. Although a joint line, the GWR was the dominant partner, as a glance at the up station building on the left reveals. The GW and GC Joint signal box, visible on the right, partly hidden by the staff-only footbridge, is also pure GWR. The main line station, which had opened as Ruislip & Ickenham in 1906, had become West Ruislip (for Ickenham) in 1947, and eventually West Ruislip. The concrete shelter on the down joint platform replaced a wider standard GWR building when the LT station was built in 1948. As with many stations in this book, this view covers a range of architectural styles from the standard GWR turn of the century brick buildings to postwar modernism. I wanted to include a view of the GW&GC Joint Line, but have included it here so that it accompanies the other coverage of the postwar LT station at West Ruislip.

Below: We are looking west along the LT platform towards Ickenham roadbridge and the Curtis building at West Ruislip. In this low level portrait, the extent of glazing, with its tall vertical panes of glass on both faces of the booking hall is apparent. Internally the booking office still remains much as Curtis had designed it, although the original platform canopy, which appears in this 1989 view, was replaced in the 1990s, as was the platform surface. Originally, the intention had been to extend the Central line to Denham, and the road bridge was constructed so that the tracks could continue under the road and parallel to the GW&GC line, and the necessary land was obtained, but this idea was later dropped, due to green belt legislation which meant that anticipated housing developments would not take place. The low roof profile of the 1962 Central Line Tube Stock, compared with conventional railway coaching stock is emphasised by the way that the door openings are faired into the roof. The modernist building at West Ruislip is important as an example of how the GWR was acting as agent on behalf of LT, and how GWR station design had evolved since Leamington Spa had been built in the late 1930s. Dr F F C Curtis become successively the Chief Architect to the Railway Executive, the BTC, and finally the British Railways Board in the 1960s. West Ruislip is in many ways the blueprint for a generation of stations from one end of BR to the other, created under his exceptionally long reign.

Above: The London & Birmingham Railway opened between Birmingham and Rugby in 1838, the principal intermediate station being Coventry. A new station replaced the original in 1840 with two through lines and two platform roads. Despite further routes to Nuneaton and Leamington, and the growth of Coventry, it remained substantially unaltered for 120 years. Electrification between Liverpool, Manchester and London hastened rebuilding work. Excavation started in January 1958 on the up side at the London end of the station for a parcels depot to replace the old depot at the opposite end of the site. Demolition of the passenger station began in August 1959, and with the removal of the old parcels depot, the twin track Warwick Road bridge was replaced by a four track bridge. Coventry No 2 signal box, near the Warwick Road bridge, was replaced in May 1960, with the new Coventry power box at the London end of the station commissioning on 14/15 April 1962. The new station was opened on 1 May 1962, about a month prior to the Queen visiting Coventry in June 1962. The visit was to open the new Cathedral, but with a Royal visit soon after the station re-opened, is often taken as the opening date. The new station was planned to relieve congestion, but no sooner had it opened, than the Beeching report recommended abandoning the Nuneaton and Leamington services, this taking place on 18 January 1965. Through trains to Leamington were reintroduced in 1977, and the Nuneaton service resumed in 1987. As we have seen, railway stations are usually a product of the architectural tastes of the day, and this was as true of Coventry as of any Victorian stations.

The station was built during Dr F F C Curtis's reign as chief architect to the Railway Executive, BTC and British Railways Board, but designed by the LM Region architects' office. We are looking from the road bridge towards Euston.

Below: The term 'Brutalist' is applied to modernist designs, and the term is mistakenly seen as a reference to the brutal way in which structures, such as the Doric Arch in London, were torn down. It originated as an amusing pun on the names of two leading Modernist architects in 1955. A friend of the husband and wife team of Peter and Alison Smithson joked that 'Brutus', as Peter had been nicknamed, and Alison were the pioneers of 'the new BrutAlism'. Because of its stark style, and the way in which much loved buildings were swept aside, many people view 1960s architecture that dominates city centres with abhorrence. George Ferguson, President of the Royal Institute of British Architects, recently commented that an X-listing of eyesore buildings should be made, with developers being given grants to replace such structures. In a media poll, Coventry station was nominated for X listing. So far, the X listing idea has not been taken up, but with the low regard in which the station is held, it is surprising that English Heritage have listed it as one of seven postwar buildings in Coventry to represent this period. We are looking from platform 2 towards Euston in November 1974.

Above: The site for Wolverhampton High Level station was acquired by the Shrewsbury & Birmingham Railway in 1847, and work on a grand entrance began two years later, but the station was not completed until 1853, when it was known as Queen Street. As the adjacent GWR station was at a lower level, the stations were colloquially referred to as High Level and Low Level, and the High Level title was officially adopted on 1 June 1885. With electrification of the West Coast Main Line, the station did not project the 1960s image that BR was keen to display, and demolition began in January 1965, although the entrance to the station drive survived. This was accorded Listed status in 1977 and sold to Wolverhampton City Council in 1986 and refurbished. The new BR station was similar to Coventry station, and provided with three through platforms, platforms 1 and 2 being separated by a middle road. An up and down goods line bypassed the station on the east side of the line. As with Coventry, the 1960s architecture has been criticised. Until 2003, the station retained its original appearance, but the revival of passenger traffic had put pressure on the three platform station, and the decision was taken to create an additional platform using the old goods line, with work being under way on a new footbridge in 2004. The 1960s footbridge predated current disabled legislation, and the work included a new access. Corus and Birse Rail were the leading contractors, which included a new 10 car platform and a two span footbridge. Access to the new footbridge was provided by three

stairwells and lift houses contained in semicircular glazed structures. We are looking towards London from platform 1 with a train of loaded HAA coal hoppers on the goods line in July 1976. Today, the scene is different with a new footbridge, an additional platform where the freight train is seen, and new canopies. Although I am not an admirer of 1960s architecture, and deplore the 1960s destruction of much of our classic railways heritage, this view demonstrates the importance of recording the contemporary railway scene. It is one of the newest stations recorded in this book, yet is now drastically altered.

Opposite top: Coventry and Wolverhampton are examples of stations serving large towns or cities, but the majority of stations served smaller places. The typical country station had a main building on one platform from Victorian times, and a shelter on the opposite platform. This pattern applied at Wool, which is west of Bournemouth on the Southampton & Dorchester Railway. It opened in 1847, the line being absorbed into the LSWR in 1848. The line from Waterloo to Bournemouth was electrified in 1966, and to facilitate through services over the non-electrified section to Weymouth, push-pull operation using Class 33 locomotives and 4-TC sets was introduced on 10 July 1967. Wool station, on the non-electrified section, was refurbished at this time, the old brick built Victorian station house on the down platform, and the wooden shelter on the up platform, being replaced by modern prefabricated units.

As many country stations were closed or reduced to an unmanned halt with the buildings sold out of railway service or demolished, Wool provides an unusual example of a country station that has been updated with modern buildings. We are looking from the footbridge towards Bournemouth in 1974. The sidings to the right are the goods yard, whilst the two sidings on the left are the remains of the World War One connection to Bovington army camp. This curved in from the left to join the sidings near the white ground frame hut visible in the distance.

Opposite bottom: General freight facilities had been withdrawn at Wool in 1967, but the reason that the up and down sidings still survived seven years later has been touched upon in the previous illustration. Wool was the nearest station to Bovington Camp, an important base for the Royal Armoured Corps, and home to the Royal Tank Museum. The Bovington camp railway had been built in the First World War, though foolishly this was lifted in 1936, three years before the outbreak of World War Two. Lacking a rail connection, traffic to and from the camp was concentrated at Wool, including movement of army vehicles on bogie Warwells and similar stock. The yard had generous end loading facilities, and stabling accommodation to cope with complete trainloads of equipment. For the modeller, Wool offers great potential, with this mix of civilian and military traffic.

Above: Shipton for Burford station lies on the Oxford, Worcester & Wolverhampton, colloquially the 'Old Worse & Worse', section of the GWR between Oxford and Kingham. It is a village in Oxfordshire with a population of 667 people in 1951, and should not be confused with nearby Shipston-on-Stour, a town of 1,500 people in Warwickshire, which was once served by a short branch from Moreton-in-Marsh. I considered whether to include this view or not. At first sight it shows very little, but that is the point. The 1956 'Handbook of Stations' lists the facilities at Shipton for Burford as G P F L H C. To railwaymen, that means the station handled Goods, Passengers, Furniture vans requiring end-loading docks, Livestock, Horseboxes and Carriage trucks by passenger train. In other words, the station was staffed, and offered a full range of facilities. All freight facilities ended in September 1965, and the station became unstaffed in January 1966. At about the same time that Wool received new buildings and waiting rooms to keep passengers out of the cold, the main buildings at Shipton were replaced with a 'bus shelter'. Paradoxically, the old GWR shelter on the opposite platform did survive, although stripped of its windows, which would have become a target for vandals now that the station was unmanned. We see the station on 27 December 1971. Wage costs meant that it was no longer economical to provide staff at small halts such as Shipton, and the mindless activities of that most loathsome

creature of modern times, the vandal, meant that waiting rooms at an unstaffed station would soon be trashed, so there was little option left to BR, but it was sad to see pretty little stations, where there had been a friendly welcome and well tended flower beds, reduced to this. The view is at sunset, which is perhaps appropriate, as the 1960s witnessed the sun setting on the traditional railway that had endured for so long.

Opposite bottom: The Victorians and Edwardians had built their railway stations to last, and in the 1930s, many important stations were barely fifty years old, such had been the pace of development in the late nineteenth century. The Big Four, confronted with road competition and the great depression at the end of the twenties, had concentrated their resources where they were most needed on more efficient motive power, new coaching stock, permanent way, and signalling improvements. From 1939 to 1945 the railways took a battering at the hands of the Luftwaffe, and through overuse and deferred maintenance. In the few years left between 1945 and nationalisation, government policy hampered refurbishment. British Railways had a backlog of work ahead of them, but before they had made any serious inroads, financial problems caught up with the rail industry, and money was diverted into the Modernisation plan, primarily towards motive power renewal, and then power signalling and electrification. Station renewals took a back seat, but with steam banished, BR sought a bright new image. The original Stevenage station, which was 28.5 miles north of Kings Cross, was built by the

GNR in 1850, and consisted of two island platforms linked by a footbridge. As Stevenage had been designated a 'New Town', and had undergone considerable expansion, the old station was no longer adequate. One option would have been to rebuild the existing station, but this would have involved ongoing disruption, and an alternative site, which was closer to the town centre, existed a mile to the south. The new station repeated the format of a pair of Island platforms linked by a footbridge. Many of the stations built during the upgrading of the West Coast Main Line prior to electrification in the Sixties, had been of prefabricated construction. They were of little merit, and unlike wine, showed no signs of improving with age. Rather than add to this dismal series of buildings, Stevenage presented a more lively approach. The station was opened by British Rail on 23 July 1973, although the formal opening by Mrs Shirley Williams MP, a long-serving Labour politician, and later a founder member of the Social Democratic Party, was not until 29 September 1973. We see the station a few months later.

Below: Three railway companies served Belfast, each with its own terminus. The LMS Northern Counties Committee served the territory north of the city from Belfast York Road station, whilst the Great Northern Railway (Ireland) stretched south to Dublin, its lines commencing at Great Victoria St. In the east, the Belfast & County Down Railway served its namesake county from Queens Quay station. A connecting line ran from the GN south of Great Victoria St to join the BCDR just outside Queens Quay. It was known as the Belfast Central Railway, and had

carried a passenger service briefly in the nineteenth century, but was latterly used for freight and occasional excursions from the GNR to Bangor on the BCDR. The only connection with the LMS NCC was via the freight lines that served Belfast harbour. The LMS NCC and BCDR were merged into the Ulster Transport Authority in 1948. The GNR(I), which had been divided between the Ulster and Southern Irish governments in 1953, was partitioned in 1958, lines in the north going to the UTA. In 1965, road widenings severed the Belfast Central link, leaving the BCDR isolated from the rest of the Irish rail network, but the absurdity of three separate under-utilised termini finally percolated through, and Northern Ireland Railways, as successor to the UTA, reinstated the Belfast Central link in the 1970s, opening a new four-platform Belfast Central station in 1976. Trains were diverted from the BCDR station at Queens Quay on 12 April, with the GN following on 26 April 1976. Although a new double track viaduct across the River Lagan was required to connect the BCDR and GN lines, a further and very costly bridge over Belfast harbour would have been needed to connect up with the former NCC section at York Road. Despite pious hopes that this would happen soon, it was not until the 1990s that a new bridge was built in conjunction with road improvements in the city, so that all lines were finally linked up. We are looking from platform 3 at the main buildings with their elevated concourse in July 1996.

Above: The Railway network was largely completed by 1914, and except for filling a few gaps, and the Southern re-developments at Ramsgate, the construction of new stations on a greenfield site, other than for minor halts such as Appleford, virtually ceased. The BRB Annual Report for 1974 revealed that, 'In the West Midlands the joint endeavours with the [Passenger Transport] Executive to obtain grant for a station to serve the National Exhibition Centre were successful and work started'. The BRB Annual Report for 1976 announced, 'Birmingham International, officially opened in September, was the first new station of major international importance to be built in Britain this century. Five years ago the site was open

farmland. The £6m station was purpose-built to serve the new National Exhibition Centre with frequent Inter-City and local trains and easy access to the central piazza within the Centre. In 1976, it was used by 35% of all visitors to the Centre'. When we visited Birmingham International, as the new station was named, on 2 July 1976, it had just opened to passengers, although the formal opening ceremony was some weeks hence, and the sign propped against the wall reveals that work was not yet finished. We are looking from platform No 1 towards Coventry.

Below: We see the Concourse on 2 July 1976. Although largely complete, a few areas still

required finishing, but I wanted to record this new station in pristine state before sustained use took its toll. Everything was immaculate, and the contractors proclaimed in their illuminated advert, 'MONK built this station'. A short message, but there was no need to say more. Although only ten years and a few miles separated Birmingham International from Wolverhampton, the extent to which architectural trends had changed is startling. In the 1940s, modernism had supplanted art deco as the Holy Grail of architecture, and BR was not immune to that trend. When Dr F F C Curtis became architect to the Railway Executive and its successors in the early days of BR, the railway industry was led by a talented architect, as is evidenced by West Ruislip, but the destruction of the Doric Arch casts a dark shadow over his long reign. To gain a balanced impression of this period, we must realise that Curtis was as much the prisoner of his time as any nineteenth century architect. Modernism, or to use the joke name that has come to haunt it, 'brutalism', is widely decried today. There were undoubted mistakes, as the vision of the modernist architects who saw a bright new future, if the old was ruthlessly swept away, was mistaken. In the 1960s, Bernard Kaukas was Principal Assistant to Dr Curtis, and later became Chief Architect to the BRB, and subsequently Director – Environment. Birmingham International was built during the Kaukas years, and reflects a move away from the more stark aspects of brutalism. The change of title to Director – Environment also revealed a growing awareness within BR of the important architectural heritage the railways possess. An example of this concerned Kettering station. In 1978, BR proposed to demolish the original MR canopies

dating from 1858, but local conservationists met with Bernard Kaukas, and he agreed that the ironwork would be preserved and the canopies repaired.

Above: When the Mersey Railway was formally opened by H R H Prince of Wales, later King Edward VII, between Rock Ferry in the Wirral and Liverpool on 20 January 1886, the Liverpool terminus was at James St, not all that far from Liverpool Pier Head and the docks. In 1892, the line was extended to terminate below the CLC station in Liverpool, the new terminus being known as Liverpool Central (Low Level). In the 1970s, the Mersey Railway was upgraded as a part of a major refurbishment of rail links on Merseyside. Birkenhead Hamilton Square station, with its tall hydraulic pumping tower, appeared as the frontispiece. James St was similarly blessed, but the tower was destroyed during the German blitz in World War Two. A new multi-story block was erected on the site, and we see the exterior of James St station with its BR arrows and Merseyside M logo in 1994. Although the central area stations of London Transport are underground, with offices or shops built at ground level, only a handful of BR stations come into this category.

Right: The upgrading of the lines on Merseyside saw the closure of the former LYR Liverpool Exchange station, with trains from the north of Liverpool being diverted via a new tunnel to join up with the former CLC line serving the south side of the city. For the Mersey Railway, the terminal at Central Low Level was replaced by a loop line, which would diverge off the existing line just short of James St station, and then run via a new platform at James St and past

two new stations at Moorfields and Lime St to Central, and then back to James St. Construction of the Loop line began in 1971, and was opened to passengers on 9 May 1977, although the formal opening by H M The Queen was not until October 1978. Merseyrail unit 508 108 is at the new 1977 platform at James St in June 1994. The loop line led to a marked increase in travel on the Mersey Railway as passengers appreciated the convenience of being able to board or alight from trains at four different points in the inner city area, and the convenient connections with the main

passenger station at Lime St. Flooding is always a problem with any underground system, but in the case of the Mersey railway, the decline in heavy industry on Merseyside has meant a dramatic reduction in the amount of water extracted by private industrial boreholes in the Liverpool area, with a slow but steady rise in the level of the water table below Liverpool, which had been artificially lowered by industrial demand for much of the nineteenth and twentieth centuries. As we have become more green, the Mersey Railway has suffered more from flooding !

Opposite top: The London, Chatham & Dover Railway was a late-comer to London, opening to the original Blackfriars passenger station on the south bank of the Thames in June 1864. The LCDR had parliamentary powers to cross the Thames, and run via Ludgate Hill (which opened later in 1864) to join the Metropolitan Railway at Farringdon St, the connection to the Met opening in 1866. The original Blackfriars station handled passenger and freight, but was so cramped that a second bridge was added over the Thames, and a new passenger station replaced it on the north bank of the river. This opened on 10 May 1886, and was known as St Paul's until 1937, when it was renamed Blackfriars. Because of its curious history, St Paul's/Blackfriars was part terminus, and part through station, a further line to Snow Hill station, later Holborn Viaduct Low Level, being added in 1874. The birth of the Underground and the growth of tram and bus services robbed the northern extensions of much of their purpose, and Low Level station closed in 1916, ending through passenger traffic on the city line. This remained a busy North-South freight link, until it was closed in 1969, and the tracks lifted two years later. By the 1980s, the Greater London Council was pressing for a North-South cross-city link, and the BRB Report for 1985/86 noted, 'The scheme for a new cross-London link by re-opening the Snow Hill tunnel between Farringdon and Blackfriars was authorised. Through running of trains between North and South of the Thames will open up new journey possibilities for customers and make better use

of rolling stock'. The new cross-London Thameslink service began in May 1988, attracting 20,000 passengers a day in its first year, but further changes soon ensued. We are looking from platforms 3/4 at Blackfriars towards Snow Hill tunnel in August 1991. The stone pillar on the right is part of the old LCDR station. The differing trainshed over the terminal roads on the right, platforms 1–3 and the through platforms 4 and 5, is noteworthy.

Opposite bottom: Part of the Snow Hill project included closing the old line over Ludgate Hill into Holborn Viaduct station north of Blackfriars, a replacement line dropping steeply from Blackfriars to a new station that was briefly called 'St Paul's Thameslink', but was renamed 'City Thameslink' to avoid confusion with St Paul's station on the Underground. We are looking north from platform No 5 at Blackfriars, and see how the line drops down to burrow beneath London, instead of being carried above street level. Thameslink trains continue north onto the Midland main line, replacing the Bedford – St Pancras, or 'Bedpan' service. With a 15% annual increase in traffic, expansion became urgent. 'Thameslink 2000' envisaged new through services via Snow Hill tunnel north to Peterborough, Cambridge and Kings Lynn, and south to Guildford, Eastbourne, Ashford and Dartford. Apart from major alterations at London Bridge, the changes at Blackfriars were to be dramatic. The station was to be remodelled with four through platforms, which would be extended across the river, with

glass screens to shelter passengers, a new passenger access being added south of the river. Because of the effect on the Thames, the proposal was controversial, and was rejected by the government in 2003. In October 2006, the Department for Transport accepted a revised scheme that would see the station spanning the river as before. Welcomed by Network Rail, it has been opposed by conservationists, due to the destruction that will be wrought to the historic Borough Market area south of the Thames. The project is estimated to cost £3.5bn and take seven years to complete.

Above: We are looking towards the buffers of platforms 1–3. With five platforms, Blackfriars is small for central London, a legacy of the late arrival of the LC&DR in the capital. Track revision at Blackfriars led to alterations to the ridge and furrow trainshed. The position of the columns with their attractive cast capitals marks the position of the old platforms, the columns between the modern tracks 2 and 3 once resting on a narrow middle platform. With the removal of the platform, the columns were extended downwards with new baseplates. Once, all three platforms were narrow with a single track between them, which was an extravagant arrangement for a cramped site. The old platform between Tracks 2 and 3 has been demolished, and the lines moved closer together. As a result, the platform between tracks 1 and 2 has been widened to the left, whilst the platform we are standing on, has been widened to the right.

Above: Convinced that London Bridge station was remote from the central area, the South Eastern Railway extended its main line by costly viaducts amongst the rooftops of the built-up south bank of the Thames to Hungerford Bridge, where it crossed the river to terminate at Charing Cross station, the terminus opening on 11 January 1864. With the replica Eleanor Cross, which is the datum point for measuring distances in London, in the forecourt, the SER achieved its goal of a central station, but at the expense of a cramped site with just six platforms. A crescent trussed trainshed was designed by Sir John Hawkshaw, but collapsed in December 1905, with the loss of six lives. A replacement transverse ridge and furrow roof was installed, which served until the late 1980s, when it was removed to make way for an air-rights development of office accommodation over the platforms. For many years, BR had relied on contributions from sales of redundant property through the British Rail Property Board, but with tighter government spending limits, this was vital if modernisation was to be funded in the 1980s. If air-rights were sold above a major London terminus, the return could be substantial. The BR Annual Report for 1987/88 commented, 'Work started on 16 other schemes including two more major projects to build office blocks over London stations. The £95m Victoria Phase II development will produce 480,000 sq ft and the £117m Charing Cross scheme a further 506,000 sq ft of offices'. Terry Farrell & Partners were the architects selected to create a striking post-modernist office block, called Embankment Place, which was completed in 1990. Unlike most office blocks that have been erected on stations, the curving roofline at Charing Cross development recaptures the image of a great trainshed, whilst the styling has definite overtones of the Southern 'Odeon' architecture of the 1930s.

Left: For many years, BR relentlessly obliterated all traces of the former companies and their initials, but as a greater respect for heritage developed, some of the old signs came back, but few would have predicted that an office block with Southern overtones would have arisen above a great London terminus, or that the letters SR would proclaim this gateway to the towns and cities of the South Coast, or that the heraldry of a past age, with the emblems of the towns served from Charing Cross, would reappear. Ordinarily I am no supporter of modern architecture, but I believe that the BR Property Board and Terry Farrell deserve credit for creating a striking new look at a station that had not looked its best since the 1905 disaster.

Right: Hastings, the newest station in this book, had not been formally opened when we photographed it in September 2006. It is a post modernist structure with an exceptionally fine passenger environment. The first station in the town opened in 1851, and served the SER and the LBSCR. Both companies had separate platforms, the SER running from Tunbridge Wells to Rye and Ashford, whilst the Brighton side was for trains terminating at Hastings on the coastal branch from Lewes. The fusion of the LBSCR and SECR into the Southern in 1923 provided an opportunity to revamp many stations where the LBSCR, SER and LCDR had been in competition. At Hastings, a new station in Southern New Classical style was constructed in 1931, the architect being J R Scott. The main building was in Wealden brick with cream stone dressings, a flat roof, and terracotta capping. The booking hall was octagonal, an innovative idea, and was provided with a matching octagonal roof light, and large round headed windows. The passage to the platforms was also illuminated by a roof lantern, and until the 1960s, the tiled booking hall boasted a Latin-American Art Deco frieze, portraying children with buckets and spades, other seaside scenes, and a Southern Electric set. It was opened for traffic on 6 July 1931. The octagonal design gave Hastings historic significance, but this was not appreciated locally, and the building was not a listed structure. Whilst it could have been properly cared for, it was allowed to deteriorate to a point where Hastings Council, the government, Network Rail, South Eastern Trains, and the South East England Development Agency all wanted it demolished to make way for a modern building that is supposed to 'breathe life' into the town. To preclude intervention by any conservationist who opposed the loss of the town's architectural heritage, Railtrack obtained a rare immunity from listing for the station, to block any last minute attempt to save the building, which was torn down in 2004.

Bottom: Hastings station, with its Southern Railway signal box and new Railtrack station buildings, reflects different architectural tastes over the past eighty years. Although I have deplored the loss of the Southern building, the new structure is impressive and is a graphic reminder of how railway architecture has always reflected the changing tastes and priorities over time. We cannot know what tomorrow may hold, but it will be of interest. We are looking towards St Leonards in September 2006.

GLOSSARY

Acanthus Leaf	Thick leafy pattern used in decoration, especially on Corinthian Capitals
Arch, elliptical	Arch in the form of an ellipse or curve that changes radius from gentle to sharp
Arch, four centred	Pointed arch, sharply curved at base, becoming shallow towards apex
Arch, round headed	A semi circular arch
Arch, segmental	Shallow arch where diameter is much greater than the width of the opening
Art Deco	Architectural style in 1930s, derived from Bauhaus thinking
Art Nouveau	Design style from c1890, decorative, sometimes fanciful
Ashlar	Large smoothly finished and finely jointed squared blocks of stone (also dressed)
Balustrade	An openwork parapet held up by balusters, usually stone, but can be decorative iron
Bargeboard	A board attached to the edge of a roof. May be decorated
Barley Twist	A twisted pattern said to resemble a barley stick sweet
Bedstone	A large stone or concrete block on which a structure rests
Brutalist style	Nickname for post-1945 Modernism, from architects 'Brutus' and Alison Smithson
Campanile	Italian style tower, shallow hipped roof and round headed windows (see Gobowen)
Capital	The top of a column, can be Greek or Roman, Doric, Corinthian, Ionic or Tuscan
Clerestory	The central raised section of a roof with glazing to provide good lighting
Corbel	A projection from a wall, which can be decorative or used to support a beam
Corinthian Capital	A decorative top to a fluted column, usually decorated with Acanthus leaves
Cornice	A projecting moulding at the top of a wall or arch
Cottage Orne	Architectural style resurrected c1900; rustic, half timbering, ornate bargeboards
Crenellated	Resembling the high and low portions of a battlement on a castle
Cresting	Ornamental work at top of a roof, esp. common on French Chateau style buildings
Cupola	A small dome crowning the top of a tower or turret
Dentils	A row of small regularly shaped projecting blocks beneath a cornice
Domestic Revival	Architectural style popular from 1880s to 1920s, step pitch roofs, overhanging eaves
Doric Capital	A decorative top to a fluted column, usually plain or ringed (Greek or Roman)
Dressed	Large smoothly finished and finely jointed squared blocks of stone (also Ashlar)
Extrados	The upper surface of an Arch
Finial	An ornamental spike or ball on top of a roof or post
French Renaissance	Chateau style, steep pavilion roofs with iron cresting — see Langley
Gable roof	A roof where one or more ends is in the form of a vertical triangle
Gable wall	A Dutch gable has upper sides shaped with curved line often rising to a small pediment
Gable wall	A stepped (or crow stepped) gable rises in the form of a flight of steps
Georgian	Classical Architecture, rectangular often with pediments, developed after 1714
Gothic	Highly decorative with ecclesiastical traditions, pointed arch, popular mid-19th century
Hipped roof	A roof with sloping ends rather than vertical gables
Intrados	The lower surface of an arch
Ionic Capital	A decorative top to a fluted column, usually decorated with spirals
Italianate style	Architectural style with round headed windows, square towers, shallow hipped roofs
Jacobean style	Revival of James II architectural style, curly gables, tall chimneys
Keystone	The wedge shaped topmost stone in an arch
Lancet window	Tall narrow window with a pointed arch top
Lattice girder	A girder consisting of top and bottom horizontal flanges connected by X pattern strips
Masonry	Work built by a mason out of stone, also used for brick
Modernism	Architectural style from c1945 to 1980s, rectangular uncompromising concrete style
Mullion	A narrow vertical stone pillar dividing a window
Odeon Style	Southern Railway concrete architecture in 1930s, allegedly similar to cinema design
Oriel Window	A projecting bay window on an upper floor
Pediment	Curved or triangular shape above a door, window, portico or gable
Pilaster	A flat or square column projecting slightly from a wall but joined to it
Porte Cochere	A porch, usually glazed, at the front of a building under which vehicles unload
Quatrefoil	Four lobed cut out decoration
Queen Anne	Architecture in style used in reign of Queen Anne 1702–1714. See Market Harborough
Quoins	Decorative stones, alternately long and short at the edge of a building
Rough Hewn	Also Rock Faced stone; stone as cut at quarry and not given smooth dressing
Running-In board	A large nameboard at the end of the platform seen by passengers as the train arrives
Rusticated	Large square blocks of stone, with prominent deep joints, various surfaces often rough
Soffit	The lower surface of an arch, architrave or canopy
Spandrel	A bracket projecting from a wall and supporting a projecting canopy. Often decorative
Stanchion	An upright iron or steel support, often for railings
String Course	A decorative horizontal band of brick or stone along a wall
Terracotta	A high quality hard brick or tile, often highly decorated and glazed
Transom	A horizontal bar across a window, see also Mullion
Trefoil	Three lobed cut out decoration, resembles a three leaf clover
Truss	Roof support of timber, iron or steel
Tudor style	Henry VIII (1509–1547) architecture, straight gables, tall decorated chimneys
Tuscan Capital	A top to a plain column, with little decoration
Valance	The decorative vertical edging timber on a canopy
Weatherboarding	Horizontal wood cladding with boards overlapped from above to protect from rain